Guidelines for the documentation of computer software for real time and interactive systems

**2nd edition
1990**

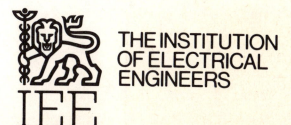

THE INSTITUTION
OF ELECTRICAL
ENGINEERS

IEE

Published by: The Institution of Electrical Engineers, London

© 1990: Institution of Electrical Engineers

ISBN 0 86341 233 5

Printed in the United Kingdom

List of Contents

Preface

This second edition of the IEE Guidelines for the Documentation of Computer Software for Real Time and Interactive Systems adds to the information included in the first edition, revises other information in the light of technological developments and includes changes based on comments on the first edition. Additional sections provide guidance on feasibility studies and their documentation, on quality assurance and on documentation management.

The title of the Guidelines has been changed to reflect their applicability to a wider range of systems. It should be noted that a considerable portion of the Guidelines is also relevant to the documentation of commercial and business systems.

This publication provides guidance on the documentation required for the acquisition, operation and maintenance of software for real time and interactive computer-based systems. Its scope is wide-ranging, dealing as it does with the documentation of feasibility studies, users' requirements, suppliers' functional specifications, software system specifications and system acceptance testing, as well as the documentation of the software itself. The concluding sections cover the way in which documentation should be controlled, changed, developed and managed.

Inevitably, the scope of a publication of this nature has to be limited to some degree, and such topics as the software selection process, software engineering methods and hardware documentation are not covered, although aspects of hardware having an influence on software are mentioned.

A glossary of technical terms is included.

The reader's attention is drawn to the detachable page at the back of the Guidelines. Comments on the content and usefulness of this publication are invited and should be returned to the editor at the address given.

Acknowledgements

This revision and extension of the Guidelines for the Documentation of Software in Industrial Computer Systems published in 1985 has been carried out by a Working Party of the Computing Standards Sub-Committee (now the Information Technology Standards Sub Committee) within the Computing and Control Division of the Institution of Electrical Engineers with editorial assistance from Messrs C. D. Marsh and D. A. Kemp of the Institution's Technical Affairs Department.

The Working Party consisted of the following members:

Mr R. J. Scott-Kerr (Independent Systems Consultant) Chairman
Mr P. P. Docherty (CEGB) representing the British Computer Society
Dr R. T. Herrod (Solvit Scientific Engineers)
Mr M. J. Pilditch (Computer Sciences Company)
Mr J. B. Stewart (Civil Aviation Authority)
Mrs J. Thornton (Ferranti International).

Further valuable advice was obtained from the members of a Consultative Committee set up to represent a broad spectrum of expertise across the industry.

The IEE is grateful for the time and effort spent by all concerned in the production of the Guidelines. It is believed that the Guidelines will make a valuable contribution for both suppliers and users towards improving the quality and effectiveness of real time and interactive computer-based systems.

Section One: Introduction to the Guidelines

1.1 Readership of the Guidelines

The use of computers in industry and commerce has become an essential element of modern life. This increasing dependence on computer systems has brought to light the lack of guidance for users on the documentation needed for successful acquisition, development, operation and maintenance of real time and interactive computer-based systems. This publication aims to provide that guidance.

The Guidelines will be of particular assistance to small and medium-sized companies and software suppliers with little experience in introducing such systems. However, larger companies, established software and equipment suppliers, consultants and educationalists should also find this publication a useful and comprehensive guide to the subject.

1.2 Scope and purpose of the Guidelines

To avoid the many pitfalls that can hinder or prevent a successful system implementation, it is essential to ensure effective communication between the user and the supplier, bearing in mind that each will be operating in his own highly specialised area of expertise and may not be familiar with the other's specialisation. Companies with little or no experience in introducing real time and interactive computer-based systems are unlikely to be able to foresee all the potential problems of software specification and procurement. Similarly, software suppliers with little experience in the user's application may fail to appreciate all the requirements of such systems. Software suppliers are also advised to consider the NCC STARTS *Guide to methods and software tools for the construction of large real time systems* which provides guidance in other areas not covered in this Guide (see Section 11, Bibliography).

An essential element in achieving effective communication is the provision of accurate, complete and timely documentation at each stage of the project. The Guidelines describe the documentation required at each stage, from the feasibility study and initial specification to the operation of the installed system. Detailed attention is given to all software aspects of the documentation: hardware topics are discussed only where they cannot easily be separated from software considerations.

The Guidelines do not define document layout and presentation. Instead, the emphasis is placed on documentation content, and on the need for complete, clear, precise and unambiguous statements of requirements, specifications and procedures. Particular stress is laid on the importance of formal agreements between user and supplier and on the need for rigorous control of changes. The Guidelines do not cover source code, or give guidance on good coding practice or conventions. Advice is given on the key factors of documentation management that support the production of good documentation. An example model entitled *Software Quality Assurance: Model Procedures* is also published by the IEE.

The Guidelines contain a number of checklists to ensure that no major topic is overlooked. While these checklists may not be exhaustive, they are sufficiently comprehensive to be applicable to the most complex projects; for simple projects, an appropriate selection of items can be made.

Detailed discussion of contractual procedures and considerations has been omitted, although the contractual importance of certain software-related documents and events is emphasised.

The Guidelines contain a bibliography which lists public standards that have been found relevant to software documentation.

Since it has not been possible to cover the subject without using technical terms, a glossary is provided.

1.3 Application to different types of system

Computer systems for real time and interactive applications comprise a wide range of hardware, firmware and software components, configured in varying degrees of complexity to provide systems of an equally varied range of function and cost. Such systems included communications network control and industrial control applications such as sequence control, automatic control, data acquisition and monitoring.

In the Guidelines, systems have been classified according to their complexity, thus:

Fixed Program System (FPS)

Limited Variability System (LVS)

Full Variability System (FVS).

Typically fixed program systems are standard products with no facility for functional variation by individual users; limited variability systems are more flexible, with some facility for variation to meet individual requirements; full variability systems are complex systems specially produced for particular users, with potential for future modification by the user to meet changing needs. The characteristics of these systems are described in more detail in *1.3.1* to *1.3.3* below.

Throughout the Guidelines, advice is given on the documentation requirements for each of the system classifications. Thus, whilst comprehensive guidance is given for the more complex systems, users contemplating the purchase of systems in the simpler categories will be able to select the most advantageous approach to meet their particular needs.

The Guidelines describe all the aspects of the documentation of a system's software that should be considered by the user. It is not implied that a formal document is necessarily produced under each heading. In some cases this would be superfluous, in others it would impose a cost penalty on the project that could not be justified on the grounds of functionality, maintainability, availability or future system development potential. The user should, however, bear in mind that the production of adequate design and development documentation is essential to the successful implementation of any computer system. He may consider using the documentation management practices and the documentation standards and procedures of any potential supplier as one measure of the likely quality of the final system. Suppliers should be expected to produce documentation according to the Guidelines, as indicated in Figure. 2 (Page 1-9).

Although documentation is a fundamental component of computer systems, the cost of good documentation is far from negligible. The user should, therefore, consider the likely cost before requesting additional documentation outside his particular needs. At the same time the cost implications and effects of not having the optimum level of documentation to meet present and future needs should not be underestimated.

Where a real time system is to be developed, it may not be clear, initially, which functions are to be performed by hardware alone and which are to be performed in part by software. In these early stages of specification and design, it is recommended that these Guidelines are applied to the whole system. When the functions are separately identified, then the appropriate guidance from this publication may be applied to the documentation of the software.

1.3.1 Fixed program system

This type of system is represented by the many proprietary, dedicated-function systems which are available as standard off-the-shelf products.

Examples are

Network controllers

Automatic controllers

Sequence controllers

Small data logging systems.

These products may emulate, and in some cases be interchangeable with, other established equipments.

Normally the supplier will sell fixed program systems as single standard products or as a limited range of products with compatibility restricted to items within the range. The functional specification of the FPS will be fixed and will normally be documented in the supplier's data sheets, catalogues and the like. The user will be unable to alter the function of the product. Instead he will be limited to the adjustment of a few parameters to enable the system to be matched to external interfaces.

Most of the documentation for this type of system will consist of standard publications from the supplier. It is likely to prove costly if the user insists on documentation tailored to his individual needs, and in most cases this will prove unnecessary.

1.3.2 Limited variability system

A limited variability system is a more flexible system which provides the user with some capability for adjusting it to his own specific requirements. The system functions will normally be configured by the use of an application-related language or diagrammatic method, and will not necessarily require the specialist skills of the computer programmer.

Limited variability systems are usually built from a standard range of hardware and software components. Some suppliers offer a range of such systems, each aimed at a particular application area, which can be interconnected to form complex distributed systems.

Each LVS in a supplier's range should have a comprehensive specification which defines the basic functional components and the method of configuring them into a system. In addition, some application-specific documentation will be required, describing how the system is actually configured.

1.3.3 Full variability system

Typically, a full variability system will be a computer-based system equipped with an operating system which provides system resource allocation and a real-time multi-programming environment. The system will be tailored for a specific application by computer specialists, using high level languages such as Ada, C, CORAL, BASIC, FORTRAN, Pascal, or lower level languages as necessary.

An FVS will often be unique for a specific application and will be produced on a one-off or very low volume basis. As a result, with the exception of the supplier's standard documentation for the operating system, any standard application packages and programming languages, most of the documentation will be special-to-project and therefore of significant cost. However, the user should bear in mind that inadequate documentation quality has, in the past, been a major cause of difficulty in achieving successful implementation of these more powerful and complex systems.

1.4 Definitions and Terminology

For simplicity, the terms **user** and **supplier** have been used throughout the Guidelines. In practice, the term **user** could imply purchaser, customer, owner, plant manager, agent, client or employed consultant. The term **supplier** could likewise imply manufacturer, vendor, contractor, sub-contractor, systems house, user company's own systems department, consultant, software designer or systems designer. The pronoun **he** should be understood to refer equally to men and women. A number of variations have arisen in the titles accorded to the various types of documentation. The following titles have been used in the Guidelines:

Feasibility Study Report. The report produced as the outcome of a study to identify and analyse the problems associated with an outline proposal for a system development project in order to demonstrate its viability, costs and benefits.

User Requirements Specification. A statement by the user of his total requirements.

Tender. A supplier's response indicating his proposal for meeting all the user's specified requirements.

Functional Specification. A document agreed between supplier and user which defines what will be provided under the contract.

Software System Specification. The supplier's documentation detailing how the software is designed to meet the requirements of the Functional Specification and describing the software system in detail.

Acceptance Testing Documentation. The supplier's documentation concerned with testing the system to demonstrate its capability of meeting the requirements of the Functional Specification.

Post-Installation Documentation. The totality of documents supplied to the user by the supplier for operational support and, where applicable, future development of the system.

1.5 Project stages and associated documentation

The stages of a software engineering project are defined as follows:

Feasibility study stage. The stage at which an initial study of the requirements is undertaken and the feasibility of a number of different approaches and solutions is studied, with estimates of resources, timescales and costs. Prototyping techniques may be considered appropriate where the user is unclear about his requirements or expectations of the system.

User requirements stage. The stage at which the user's requirements are defined in sufficiently precise detail to allow suppliers to produce tenders for the work.

Functional specification stage. The stage at which the supplier, in conjunction with the user, develops the Functional Specification, showing what functions are to be provided to meet the user's requirements, stating what resources will be required, and providing the agreed basis of the system design.

Software system specification and development stage. The stage at which the supplier specifies the detailed design of the software system, produces the program code to realise that design, tests the individual programs and integrates them into the complete software system.

Acceptance testing stage. The stage at which a series of system tests are carried out, designed to demonstrate to the user that all the requirements defined in the Functional Specification have been satisfied.

In-service support stage. The stage which covers the operational life of the system, with all the activities necessary to sustain the system to an agreed material state and at a specified level of performance.

Disposal stage. The stage at which the operational life of the system comes to an end, and the system and its associated documentation are disposed of.

Notes

Quality, documentation and configuration management activities cover the whole **system lifecycle.**

The documentation of the system is built up and refined as the project develops through its various states. For most stages of the project, the item produced as a result of the activities of the stage is a document. These document 'deliverables' form milestones in the development of the project and mark the transition from one stage to the next. See Figure 1, Page 1-8.

Not all the documentation produced by the supplier will be available to the user or required by the user. The Guidelines indicate, for each class of document:

The separate responsibilities of user and supplier

Where it is essential for the user to agree the content formally with the supplier

Which documents are required by the user to operate or maintain the delivered system

Which documents should be visible to the user as an indication of development progress.

The completed software documentation will consist of many documents created during the project life cycle. It is not possible to give detailed guidance on the sequence in which many of these documents should be produced, but it is important that design specifications are completed before work starts on the coding and testing of programs. This provides a vital check-point before work starts on the most expensive stage of the development.

The documentation associated with the project stages is outlined below. Figure 2 (p.1-9) illustrates supplier and user responsibilities for documentation.

1.5.1 Feasibility Study
(see Section 2)

The initial document defines the scope and terms of reference of the study, including operational requirements, budgetary limitations, timescales and relevant background information. The study culminates in the submission of a Feasibility Study Report which analyses the options available and recommends a solution, with supporting justification.

1.5.2 User Requirements Specification (see Section 3)

The documentation starting point must be a clear, complete and unambiguous statement of the user's requirements. The preparation of the User Requirements Specification may involve a complete reappraisal of current operations and objectives, coupled with advice from a number of suppliers on the possibilities for applying computer systems.

The requirements should be stated in measurable terms, describing the functions to be met by the system, but leaving the maximum degree of design freedom for the supplier. Writing a specification around one supplier's equipment should be avoided.

1.5.3 Functional Specification
(see Section 4)

The tendering process which normally follows the submission of a User Requirements Specification will produce a number of tender proposals from which a supplier may be selected. It is then the task of the chosen supplier, in collaboration with the user, to produce the Functional Specification.

This document defines how all the elements of the User Requirements Specification will be met by a supplied system, without entering into technical details of the design itself. If alternative schemes are presented, or if certain requirements are difficult to satisfy, a formal agreement must be reached between user and supplier as to the scheme finally chosen.

The Functional Specification, when agreed, usually becomes the main contractual document defining the design task to be carried out, the system and services to be supplied and the facilities to be made available.

For a fixed program system, the supplier will normally produce the Functional Specification internally without user involvement.

1.5.4 Software System Specification (see Section 5)

In this collection of documents, the supplier describes how each component of the software is designed and implemented. For the user, it provides a statement of the design and a means of monitoring the progress of design and development activity. It also forms the basis of the software support information which may be required as part of the user's post-installation documentation.

In its final form it should clearly relate to the individual requirements of the Functional Specification.

1.5.5 Acceptance Testing Documentation
(see Section 6)

The user should accept a delivered system only after satisfactory completion of a contractually agreed sequence of tests. It is advisable, therefore, to include in the User Requirement Specification a well-defined list of tests that are envisaged, so that potential suppliers are fully aware of the test requirements prior to tendering.

Acceptance testing documentation should include a statement of test philosophy, an agreed test plan and detailed test schedules.

1.5.6 Post-Installation Documentation
(see Section 7)

This is the documentation provided for the in-service stage of the project. It includes all the documentation required by the user to:

Understand the design principles of the delivered system

Operate the system in all modes and under all conditions

Test the system for correct operation

Reconstitute the software following loss or damage

Diagnose faults and repair the system

Train operators, management, technical and maintenance staff

Modify or develop the system.

Where software has been written specifically for a project, post-installation documentation will in most cases include technical descriptions of that software. Where standard software is supplied, the user would not normally expect to receive detailed information on its internal design.

1.6 Documentation Management
(see Section 8)

Effective management is essential to the production of good software documentation. Guidance is given on the key points of documentation management, to help users in assessing a supplier's management practices.

1.7 Configuration Management
(see Section 9)

One of the most important aspects of software and documentation management is the maintenance of complete records of issues and changes as they occur. This requires every issue of every software module and every document to be referenced unambiguously and all changes to be recorded after their approval. The term **configuration control** is sometimes used for this important subject.

1.8 Quality Assurance
(see Section 10)

Quality assurance is a planned and systematic pattern of all actions necessary to establish adequate confidence that the product or service conforms to established technical requirements. This means that adequate quality control methods are in place and effective during software development projects to fully satisfy the user's requirements.

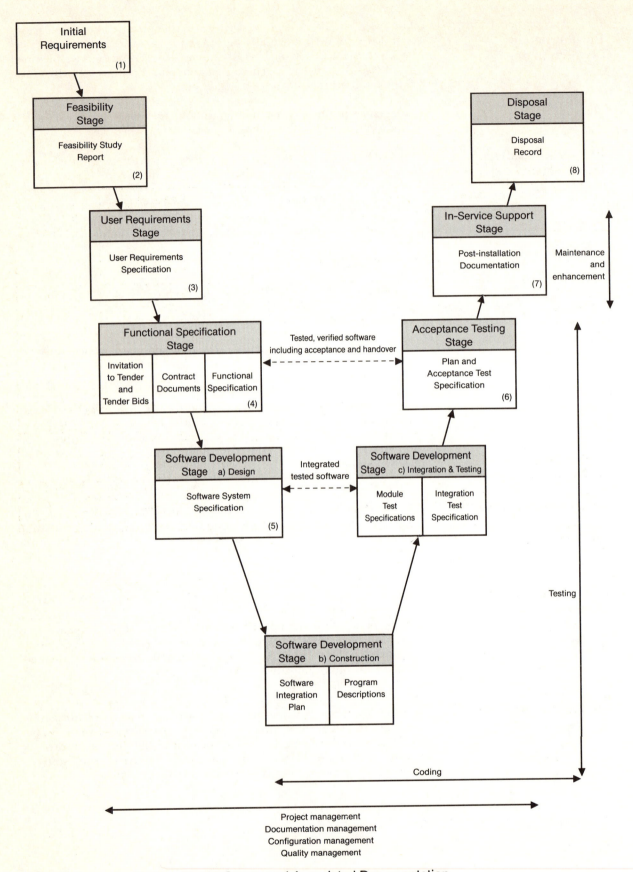

Figure 1 Computer System Project Stages and Associated Documentation
(Numbers refer to sections in text)

Project Stage Document	Feasibility Study Stage	User Requirements Stage	Functional Specification Stage	Software System Development Stage	Acceptance Testing Stage	In-Service Support Stage
Feasibility Study (2)	USER	USER				
User Requirements Specification (3)		USER	SUPPLIER + USER			
Functional Specification (4)			SUPPLIER + USER	SUPPLIER	SUPPLIER + USER	
Software System Specification (5)				SUPPLIER SUPPLIER		SUPPLIER AND/OR USER
Acceptance Test Plan and Specification (6)				SUPPLIER + USER	SUPPLIER + USER	
Post Installation Documentation (7)				SUPPLIER + USER	SUPPLIER + USER	

KEY   written by [ ]   used by [ ]

Figure 2 Supplier and User Documentation Responsibilities
(Numbers refer to sections in text)

Section Two: Feasibility Study

2.1 Purpose of the feasibility study

The feasibility study is intended to precede the commitment to select, purchase or develop new computer systems. A feasibility study is conducted when essential information and/or expert advice is needed to identify risks and alternatives and to allow decisions to be made by the users of the system.

2.1.1 Scope of the Guidelines

These Guidelines identify factors to be considered and included in the results of feasibility studies. The results should be presented in a report; a suggested format for such a report is given in Section 2.6.

2.1.2 Application to different types of system

The procedure described in this section of the Guidelines is oriented towards feasibility studies of any type of system i.e. fixed program, limited variability or full variability system.

2.2 Defining a feasibility study

A feasibility study is an investigation directed to find and evaluate acceptable solutions to a problem. In system terms this may include an appraisal of currently available hardware and software, leading to a recommendation of the most suitable system. The general objectives of a feasibility study are usually to:

Identify, within a broad-based study, functions of the organisation where operational or financial benefit can be obtained from the introduction of new or replacement systems

Identify and define problem areas, including potential hazards

Establish the options and the financial feasibility of new or replacement systems

Define the benefits and impact of proposed systems

Define effects on other systems—both side effects and drawbacks

Assess the risks involved in development and likely timescales for the production and commissioning of an operational system

Assess the operational, safety, and security risks associated with possible new systems

Identify a likely system lifetime

Recommend a course of action.

2.2.1 Terms of reference

All objectives should be stated clearly in terms of reference drawn up at the start of the study and should be agreed with the user. The purpose of the terms of reference is to provide an initial definition of what is to be done during the feasibility study. It may be necessary later to revise the terms, particularly if the user is uncertain about the objectives. However, it is important at the start of the survey to outline constraints within the terms of reference and to get written approval for them from the user. These may include:

Operational requirements

Budgetary limitations

Timescales

Level of user sophistication

Other relevant factors.

It is also important to include in the terms of reference a broad description of how the study is to be carried out and an outline of the work to be done, giving timescales and an indication of the level of detail required as determined by the objectives.

2.3 Problem analysis

The objective of the analysis is to state the main functions of the proposed system or service. It is important to ensure that the statement of the problem is defined at an early point in the study and that it is understood and agreed by the user. To achieve this, the investigator should:

Identify how existing procedures operate and thus increase understanding

Carefully note any deficiencies in the existing procedure

Identify what functions are missing and for what reason

Undertake fact-finding relating to the present user organisation

Determine data availability

Identify the main data flows.

When requirements become clearer, objectives for the new system(s) should be defined. Formal agreements should be obtained with the user as to what the system shall and shall not do (i.e. the statement of intent).

An interview schedule with accompanying notes should be established. People chosen for interview should be interviewed in an organisational 'top-down' order. Requirements identified by subordinates should be referred back to their managers for agreement.

2.4 Options

From the requirements, possible options should be identified and listed. These may include:

Use of the existing system

Use of suitable packages on existing or new hardware

Use of systems used by other organisations in similar circumstances

Tailoring of a general purpose system

Design and development of software for the user

For hardware, the use of mainframe, mini, micro or a network/distributed processor and/or special purpose hardware.

During the selection of candidate solutions, checklists should be used. These checklists may contain such questions as:

What function, service or role will the system play?

When more than one objective is identified, which are the more important?

What throughput is needed, e.g. message rate, frequency of process transactions, batch frequencies, etc?

What are the inputs and outputs of the system?

Who is responsible for the inputs and who will receive the outputs?

What are the project's financial and time constraints?

What constraints exist for change-over to a new system (e.g. compatibility, standards, physical site considerations)?

What processing is to be done in real time, on-line or batch mode; what response times and availability are necessary?

What savings or manpower, materials or equipment utilisation are expected?

Does software availability limit the choice of hardware?

What level and type of support is needed from manufacturers, suppliers and third parties?

What features are needed for security, system lifespan, growth?

2.4.1 Technical feasibility

An assessment of the technical feasibility of selected solutions should indicate to what extent they meet the objectives. The assessment should cover:

The relative technical merits of the selected options in terms of performance, availability, capacity, etc. (Include the benefits of each, quantifiable and non-quantifiable)

Reliability

User interface

Time taken to become operational

Any trade-off decisions which are required

Technical risk assessment

Management and support requirements to run the candidate solution.

2.4.2 Financial feasibility

This should cover:

The capital and running costs for the selected solution. (The method of assessing capital costs should be in line with normal practice in the industry concerned.)

The compared cost of the proposed solution against continued use of the previous or current system, if any

Estimated costs for each of the following, where appropriate:

requirements specification

system design

programming

hardware

certification

implementation

operations

maintenance

training

accommodation

installation

organisation

staffing

2.4.3 Timescale feasibility

An outline development plan should be prepared. As a minimum this should consist of a task/activity list together with an annotated master schedule.

2.5 Recommended solution

For the chosen option, further detail should be produced to substantiate the recommendation. To supplement the information described in Section 2.4.2, the following costing checklists should generally be included:

(a) **Equipment requirements**

Equipment configuration (e.g. computers, power supplies, networks, lines, terminals, magnetic media, storage cabinets, furniture)

Equipment environment (e.g. any air conditioning and power supply requirements)

Equipment acquisition programme

Equipment installation or conversion

Equipment maintenance.

(b) **User manpower requirements** (system development)

Requirements specification

Functional specification

System design and specification

Program implementation

Testing and acceptance

System documentation and/or clerical procedures, development and training

Data transfer from existing system

Parallel running and cutover to new system

Training.

(c) **User manpower requirements** (system operation)

Running the non-computer parts of the system

Data preparation

Control of input and output documentation

Security and audit

Equipment operation

Equipment maintenance

Software maintenance

Training.

(d) **Space requirements**

People

Equipment

Spares

Supplies

Files.

(e) **Time requirements**

Conduct studies

Prepare and distribute invitations to tender

Evaluate bids and select supplier(s)

Negotiate contracts

Order, progress and install equipment

Test and acceptance

Develop and implement the system, perhaps in several phases.

2.5.1 Benefits

The way in which and degree to which the organisation/user should benefit from the recommended course of action should be set out. Where benefits are quantified, any assumptions should be clearly stated.

Benefits should be defined in two categories:

Tangible

Intangible

(a) **Tangible benefits.** These are benefits which result directly from implementation of the recommended solution. They include

Savings on manpower

Savings in employed capital; equipment utilisation

Increased productivity

Savings on running costs

Improved quality

Increase in operational data, leading to improved utilisation, throughput or reduced future investment.

(b) **Intangible benefits.** Examples include:

Decreased risk

Indirect savings through improved information process accuracy, availability and timeliness

Better and more efficient procedures

It should be noted that during any evolution, transition or replacement, there may be disbenefits or penalties such as temporary loss of facilities. Any study should pay regard to the impact of the installation of the system on the business in general.

2.5.2 Performance of selected option over objectives

Where the conclusions drawn from the study indicate that a new or revised system should be developed and implemented, a checklist should be applied to compare the selected option against the objectives. Typical questions to be asked are:

Are the system requirements identified?

Are the functions to be served specified and are principal output requirements given at a realistic level of detail?

Have the constraints under which the selected option will operate been stated?

Is an outline design solution described?

Are inputs, main processes, interactions and estimated hardware requirements given?

Does the solution meet the constraints which apply?

Is an outline development plan included?

Have estimates been given for resources required and timescales?

Are cost estimates given for development stages and system operation?

Are the benefits of the new system made clear?

What are the risks? Consider

Level of support available from suppliers of hardware and software

Solvency of companies supplying hardware and software

Technical innovation

Are products established or are they just promises?

Development over-run (time and cost)

Failure to meet performance

Security threats

User's ability to absorb and maintain the new system.

2.6 Structure of the Feasibility Study Report

The following structure is suggested for the Feasibility Study Report:

Introduction

Management summary

The problem

Analyses of options

Recommendations

Support material.

2.6.1 Introduction

This section is intended to give a brief background to the task. It should state:

What the document is

For whom it is written, by whom, and how its production was authorised and initiated

Its purpose

Its bases, the study team's terms of reference and how the study was carried out

Its structure and method of use and how it should be read

Specific acknowledgements for assistance and support.

2.6.2 Management summary

This section should summarise the problem to be solved, the criteria for the acceptability of any proposed solution and the main recommendations of the study team. These recommendations should include a clear statement of:

The impact of the system on the working environment of its users and operators and on the people affected by its operation

Cost differences between the present and proposed systems

Quantifiable benefits of the proposed system

Other benefits of the proposed system which are not quantifiable in monetary terms

Major resource requirements, timescale and risks of the proposed system

Major recommendations, including a summary of the decision required and the actions to be effected.

2.6.3 The problem under investigation

The section should:

Describe the problem being studied

State, in detail, the criteria for the acceptability of any proposed solution which may have been set by or agreed with the user

State any constraints which are to be observed by any solution

Describe the methods used in carrying out the study

Briefly summarise options identified and considered.

2.6.4 Analyses of options

Each possible solution identified and considered should be analysed. (A feasibility study is intended to explore alternatives and to derive evidence for a choice from amongst them).

A separate section should be included in the report for each option considered. It should state:

How the option would work

What resources would be required (equipment, buildings, manpower, etc.)

What organisation would be required to operate the system

What the impact would be on the working environment of all who would be affected

Each solution should be compared with criteria, resources required should be analysed and a Cost Benefit Analysis should be carried out if appropriate.

2.6.5 Comparison of options and conclusions

It is necessary to collate all the evidence for and against the various options. This evidence clarifies reasons for recommending a particular choice. Use tables and bar charts as much as possible in the presentation of this information.

2.6.6 Recommendation

The recommended solution should be identified and its benefits and costs summarised. A summarised implementation plan should be given with a statement of its expected accuracy, the period of validity, and any assumptions underlying it. The major milestones and review points should be identified.

2.6.7 Support material

Voluminous or technical material should be placed in appendices. It is advisable to include a glossary explaining any terms in the report which are used with meanings which may not be known to all of the recipients.

Examples of other appendices which may appear:

Statistics used, their source and derivation

Technical details and equipment under discussion

Costing technique used.

Section Three: User Requirements Specification

3.1 Purpose of the User Requirements Specification

The User Requirements Specification is a document written by the user in which he defines clearly and precisely what he wants the system to do and itemises any associated factors and/or constraints. The specification is given to prospective suppliers, who use it as a basis in preparing their tenders.

The specification should define the user's requirements in terms of:

Function – what the system must do, and

Interfaces – how the system will connect to and interact with the outside world.

As far as possible, the requirements should be defined in a way that will not prejudice the eventual system design. The emphasis should be on functionality rather than on possible methods of implementing those functions.

The user should beware of describing his requirements in vague terms: the specification should state the requirements completely, clearly and unambiguously. Enough detail should be given to ensure that potential suppliers do not have to make assumptions (would could, of course, be wrong). At the same time, suppliers should be encouraged to query any ambiguity or area of doubt. This is important because, in the early stages of the project at least, the User Requirements Specification is likely to be the only contractually valid statement of the user's requirements.

The user should aim to describe his requirements completely. Initial versions of the specification will almost always need to be updated as errors and omissions come to light, more information becomes available, or new requirements arise during the course of the project. However, the aim should be to achieve a correct and complete specification at the earliest possible stage: errors and omissions not discovered and dealt with before the project gets underway will undoubtedly lead to delays and (possibly heavy) excess costs later on.

To avoid the problems and costs that will be associated with any misinterpretation of the specification, attention should be given to the clarity of its presentation. It should be written in terms that will be understood both by the prospective suppliers and by the people who will in due course have to use the system. The use of illustrations and diagrams is to be encouraged.

The use of a feasibility study is recommended in cases where requirements are not clear (see Section 2 and Section 3.1.2).

The specification should be structured in a way that will allow readers to find pertinent information with ease. A suitable referencing system should be used for all the structural elements of the document, such as chapters, sections, lists, tables and figures. This is particularly important as the Functional Specification will in many cases need to bear a direct relationship to the User Requirements Specification, and cross-referencing will be necessary.

3.1.1 Contractual status

The user should take care to resolve the contractual status of the User Requirements Specification with any potential supplier in relation to the supplier's tender or Functional Specification and other tender documents. The user should be aware that a supplier may view his tender document or Functional Specification as contractually superceding the User Requirements Specification. Where this is so, the user must ensure that the final contract document interprets his requirements accurately and that any discrepancies are brought to light and resolved to his satisfaction.

It is suggested that the User Requirements Specification should require potential suppliers to provide a statement of their conformance to each specified requirement. Any deviations from the specified user requirements should be resolved before any contract is placed.

Where the Functional Specification is prepared and agreed by the supplier and user, it will normally become the authoritative contractual document.

3.1.2 Trials and prototypes

In view of the importance of the User Requirements Specification to the suitability of the solutions put forward by suppliers, great care must be given to its preparation. Indeed, the specification should not be written until a careful investigation of the feasibility of the system objectives has been carried out, either by the user's own personnel or by an independent consultant (see Section 2). Where the use of novel techniques or technology is contemplated this can take the form of a 'proof-of-concept' trial. In such a trial, features of the proposed system which could be regarded as speculative in nature can be the subject of practical demonstrations, in order to prove the concept and derive performance data which will be useful during the design stage of the project. In no way should a proof-of-concept trial attempt to meet all the objectives of the project. The trial should concentrate only on those areas of the possible solutions that require confirmation of feasibility.

Where the user is unclear of his requirements, or perhaps unaware of the likely range of options which a variety of solutions could offer, 'prototyping' can be carried out on some or all of the required system functions. This procedure involves the generation of software/hardware systems for the purpose of providing a demonstration of possible solutions to the user. The user, in turn, will assess the design(s) and, by an iterative procedure with the prototype production team, arrive at an optimum design. Prototype designs are produced without the rigour and controls that should be applied to operational software and therefore should never be considered for operational use. The only deliverable from a prototyping exercise should be a requirement/design document.

3.1.3 Scope of the Guidelines

In writing his User Requirements Specification the user must cover both software and hardware aspects of the total requirement, since hardware interfacing constraints can have a significant effect on the overall solution. However, only those hardware requirements that affect the software design are covered here.

3.2 Application to different types of system

3.2.1 Fixed program system

The critical characteristic of an FPS in relation to the user's requirements is that the software cannot be changed. The user must, therefore, consider his system requirements carefully, both for the present and as they are likely to evolve in the future, in order to ensure that the product(s) he selects will meet his needs over the planned lifetime of the system. This is of particular importance if the system is of significant cost or is intended for wide usage.

The FPS user is advised, therefore, to prepare a User Requirements Specification against which potential suppliers may recommend their products. The suppliers' data sheets should provide the information necessary for matching the requirements against the products.

3.2.2 Limited variability system

Preparation of the User Requirements Specification, to be used as a formal contractual statement of the user's expectations of the system, is a vital stage of an LVS project.

In view of the limited capacity for change inherent in an LVS, the user should anticipate, as far as possible, future needs and developments, and reflect these in the User Requirements Specification. The inherent limitation of an LVS may restrict the ability of the solution tendered to be adapted to meet the user's longer term requirements, unless those requirements are foreseen and specified at the start of the project.

3.2.3 Full variability system

A full variability system provides a greater degree of freedom for modification and expansion than is possible with an LVS. But this should not be thought of as a justification for putting less effort into the specification of requirements. In fact, a more complex system requires relatively more thought to be put into the process control and process management facilities in order to arrive, with the supplier's help, at the most cost-effective solution. A full User Requirements Specification, covering all the points discussed below, is essential.

Unless the appropriate foundations are laid at the system design stage, future enhancements are likely to be costly to implement. In addition, it should be borne in mind that subsequent changes, even if they are reductions in requirements, can be costly and may require extensive revalidation of the design.

3.3 Structure of the User Requirements Specification

The following structure is suggested for the User Requirements Specification:

Overview—providing a perspective of the system within the plant or total scheme, and indicating the overall objectives to which the system will relate (see *3.3.1* below).

System objectives—setting out in full detail the key objectives of the system as they relate to its operational requirement within the intended environment (see *3.3.2* below).

System interfaces—detailing those physical aspects of the environment with which the system must interface and which are predesigned or unalterable within the scope of the project (see *3.3.3* below).

System environment—detailing all other aspects of the system's environment which should be considered in the design of the system (see *3.3.4* below).

System attributes—specifying matters relating to system adaptability, availability, maintainability and usability (see *3.3.5* below).

Design, development and test considerations—detailing any restrictions on the design and/or implementation of the proposed system (see *3.3.6* below).

Commercial considerations—detailing requirements of a commercial nature, such as project timescales, project management, conformance to contractual requirements and acceptable costs (see *3.3.7* below).

Sections *3.3.2* to *3.3.4* deal with the functional requirements of the system and the environment into which the system must interface.

Sections *3.3.5* to *3.3.7* describe the other influencing factors that it is advisable to specify; for example, the user should carefully consider and specify any constraints on the project timescale, cost, suitability of system components or the complexity of the design. While not claiming to be comprehensive, these sections cover the most commonly specified constraints. Some of the topics discussed may seem to have no direct effect on the technical design of the software system, but experience has shown that many problems arise through their neglect. If these topics are covered in detail in the commercial documentation, there is no need to restate them in the User Requirements Specification.

3.3.1 Overview

As the supplier may be unfamiliar with the user's business or terminology, the overview is best written in plain terms. By describing the overall scheme in this way and placing it in context with any related new or existing systems, both the user and supplier are provided with a reference which should explain the technical jargon or acronyms which may be used later in the document.

A description of any systems or processes which fall outside the scope of the system being specified but with which there is some association (e.g. upstream and downstream processes) can assist the supplier in understanding the justification and importance of the requirements.

This section may also be usefully augmented by reproducing a summary and the recommendations of any feasibility study.

3.3.2 System objectives

The overall objectives of the system should be defined in terms of major functions, controls, displays, etc. In addition, it is important to include a clear statement of requirements for secondary systems such as data retrieval and alarms.

The topics to be covered fall under the headings of **System modes and functions** and **Operational requirements** (see below).

The user should take care not to specify his requirements in a manner which will limit the supplier's freedom in design philosophy, unless specific constraints are intended. It is helpful to the supplier if requirements can be classified as mandatory, preferred, optional, etc.

System modes and functions

(a) **System modes.** Identify all those modes of system operation that exhibit different functional characteristics (e.g. auto, manual, maintenance and start-up modes). Include requirements for graceful degradation of the system: identify acceptable alternative modes of control or isolation and discontinuation of any functions. Consider requirements for fallback facilities, if appropriate.

(b) **System functions.** Identify all the major functions of the system in relation to the different modes of operation. Identify any interaction between the functions.

Specify all secondary functions, such as data retrieval, alarm handling, condition monitoring and fault analysis.

Quantify the functions in measurable terms to allow validation of system performance.

Include a system overview diagram illustrating a conceptual model of the application. Ensure that the functions to be performed and the information flowing between them are clearly shown.

Operational requirements

(a) **Equipment**

Operator control consoles. Describe their purpose and physical layout, including any design objectives for new control techniques and any in-house style restrictions.

Operator input devices. These may include keyboards and switches, and devices such as light pens, touch-sensitive displays and voice input.

Visual information displays. These may include VDUs, LED displays, lamps, etc. Define detailed requirements for legibility, colour, alarms, mimics, status information and display hierarchies.

Hard copy output. Describe print requirements for event, error and fault logs, copies of VDU displays, etc. State any preference for types of printer or stationery.

Audible annunciation. Requirements in this area may range from a klaxon or siren on a noisy site to a console-based bell or bleep in a quiet environment. In all cases, control of pitch and volume needs consideration. Voice output may be cost-effective in some circumstances.

Identify ergonomic factors relating to operator comfort and efficiency, such as:

Ease of use

The size and design of keys, control knobs and switches for gloved operators

Operator reach, keyboard layout and provision of special function keys

Design of VDU consoles

Noise environment.

Specify standards where appropriate.

(b) **Timing**

Specify critical requirements for system timing, such as:

Throughput time

Response time to queries

Update of data and rate of change.

(c) **Safety and security**

Specify factors relating to the safety of personnel and of plant, including timing and responses to failure conditions arising within and outside the supplied system (see also *3.3.3(b)(i)* and *(d)(i)*.

3.3.3 System interfaces

The most critical aspects of the design of a system are usually the interfaces, where the system impinges on the outside world. There are two categories of computer system interface:

External equipment

Human.

A certain amount of flexibility can normally be allowed in the design of the human interfaces, providing, of course, the functional requirements are met. But the in-built features of plant equipment, computer peripherals and other systems will not normally permit such flexibility in design. The user should, therefore, take great care to define his equipment interfacing requirements precisely.

For each interface, the user should define the form of the data passed (analogue, digital, serial or parallel). Where the system must interface with another manufacturer's equipment, the recommendations given in sections *(a)* to *(g)* below must be given careful consideration for each data form. Where the supplier is to provide a turnkey solution (i.e. supplying the computer equipment, interfaces and plant-mounted equipment), these recommendations need be considered only in so far as the user wishes to impose design restrictions and standards on the supplier.

Where the interface is between an operator and the system, it is sufficient to define the data. It is not necessary to define the display formats, desk layouts or instrumentation at this stage, unless the equipment is outside the scope of the supplier. A general indication of the likely requirements and content of display formats should be provided if applicable.

For all human interfaces, identify the various levels of access to or contact with the system. Provide guidance on the style and complexity of the facilities to be provided for each operator category. For example, management may require output in the form of summaries, process operators may require highly interactive facilities with much detail, whilst maintenance personnel may need access to features not normally accessible by others.

A profile should be prepared for each category of individual directly or indirectly involved with the system, highlighting individual skills and responsibilities.

In all areas of electrical interface the user should consider his requirements under the following headings:

Common mode and series mode noise rejection

Common mode and differential voltage tolerance

Over-voltage and over-current protection

Intrinsic safety

Isolation.

Under the last heading the user should consider not only isolation between the computer and the plant, but also any need to maintain isolation between different plant sections.

All interfaces should be formally specified in an interface schedule. Any requirement for naming conventions should be stated. Sections *(a)* to *(f)* below indicate the topics to be covered.

(a) **Digital inputs**

  (i) **Reference.** Uniquely identify each digital signal with a suitable reference.

  (ii) **Significance.** Describe the significance of the input (plant status, alarm, event, etc.) for each state (i.e. on or off).

  (iii) **Validity.** Describe the conditions under which the input is valid (ranges, alarm limits).

  (iv) **Cross-reference.** Cross-refer to other inputs (analogue, digital and serial) where appropriate.

  (v) **Digital groups.** Further define digital groups (e.g. binary coded decimal inputs from thumbwheel switches) in terms of data format, range and strobing data (e.g. ENTER push button).

  (vi) **Physical location.** Define the physical location of the signal source and cross-refer to plant electrical schematics where appropriate.

  (vii) **Signal form.** Define the signal form (i.e. voltage or via volt-free contact) and define the digital state in appropriate terms (e.g. *closed* means *OK*. -5V means *off*, +5V means *on*).

  (viii) **Timing.** Describe whether the input is static or transient, and provide timing information as appropriate. Timing requirements can have an effect on the cost of interfacing hardware, e.g.:

    Fleeting signals may have to be latched using additional hardware until read by the software

    Resolution timing between two inputs or interfacing of pulse rates may require special hardware.

  (ix) **Response time.** Define the required response time. This should include two elements:

    Time from stimulus present to initiation of response

    Time from initiation of response to completion of process.

(b) **Digital outputs**

The interface requirements of digital outputs should be defined in similar terms to the digital input interface requirements. In addition:

(i) **Shut-down conditions.** Define the state to which outputs should revert under all failure and system shut-down conditions. Special hardware may be required to achieve this.

(ii) **Timing.** Short pulses may demand timing to a resolution beyond the computer's capability, so requiring special hardware.

(c) **Analogue inputs**

(i) **Reference.** Uniquely identify each analogue signal with a suitable reference (e.g. tag number).

(ii) **Significance.** Describe the significance of the input (e.g. flow, weight, temperature, height, speed) and the plant component to which it refers.

(iii) **Validity.** Describe the conditions under which the input is valid (ranges, alarm limits, strobing conditions).

(iv) **Cross-reference.** Cross-refer to other inputs where appropriate, and describe the conditions under which the input is valid with respect to them.

(v) **Physical location.** Define the physical location of the transducer or signal source and cross-refer to plant electrical schematics where appropriate.

(vi) **Signal form.** Define the signal form and range in terms of the electrical interface (e.g. 0-10V, 1-5V, 4-20mA) which represents zero to full scale. Define the function by which this signal range represents the data (e.g. linear, logarithmic) in engineering units (e.g. m/sec, tonnes, degrees C).

(vii) **Common mode rejection.** Clearly identify requirements for common mode rejection (many systems have limited capability).

(viii) **Sampling rate.** Define the minimum sampling or update rate for each input.

(ix) **Accuracy and resolution.** Specify the required accuracy and resolution for converting the input signal to internal units. The resolution can be expressed as the number of bits of resolution provided by the A to D Converter. The resolution and accuracy of the signal can be expressed in engineering units (e.g. 5% accuracy to 1° C resolution).

(x) **Noise characteristics.** Specify noise characteristics and filtering requirements for noisy signals. Software methods of filtering may not be feasible, in which case special hardware must be used.

(d) **Analogue outputs**

The interface requirements of analogue outputs should be defined in similar terms to the analogue input interface requirements. In addition:

(i) **Shut-down conditions.** Define the state to which all outputs should revert under all failure and system shut-down conditions.

(e) **Serial inputs and outputs**

Serial input and output interfaces are normally referred to as input/output **pairs** or **ports**. Some ports may, however, be input only or output only. Consideration should be given to the possible requirement for connection to existing or planned networks (e.g. LAN, WAN) and the adoption of the ISO Open System Interconnection (OSI) standards. In such cases, requirements should be defined in adequate detail.

For each port, provide the following information.

(i) **Reference.** Uniquely identify each serial port or channel with a suitable reference.

(ii) **Interface standard.** Specify the physical interface standard or subset used (e.g. RS232C, RS422, etc).

(iii) **Character code standard.** Specify the character code standard employed (e.g. ASCII, ISO 646) as number of bits, plus parity if appropriate, together with data-framing start and stop bits.

(iv) **Data signalling rate.** Specify the data signalling rate in baud or bits per second. Typical rates are 300, 1200, 4800 and 9600 baud.

(v) **Transmission type.** Specify the transmission types as duplex, half-duplex, input-simplex or output-simplex.

(vi) **Data flow controls and protocols.** Specify any data flow controls and protocols used and whether asynchronous or synchronous (e.g. 'X' ON-'X' OFF, HDLC). Note that certain protocols require special hardware, and that synchronous and asynchronous capabilities are not normally available on the same interface card.

The specification and function of the messages which will pass at serial interfaces (e.g. input/output with VDUs) will normally be detailed in the Functional Specification. However, if the message formats are outside the scope of the design and supply of the software to which the Functional Specification relates, full details of inputs arising and outputs required should be specified in the User Requirements Specification. This would be the case where a system was to be integrated into a network of serially connected devices where the interfacing protocols and standards had been previously laid down or certain application features had been established on the other equipment.

(f) **Local Area Networks (LAN)**

Where the use of a local area network is contemplated, its characteristics with respect to the system's functional requirements should be considered carefully. LANs are of two basic types:

Deterministic—where the throughput between communicating nodes can be guaranteed to be completed within a fixed time period not affected by network traffic (e.g. a token passing type of LAN e.g. IEEE Std 802.5);

Non-deterministic—where the throughput time cannot be pre-determined or guaranteed, being dependent on the density of network traffic (e.g. IEEE Std 802.3—Ethernet is a non-deterministic type).

Where the system is to be connected to an existing LAN, the User Requirements Specification should specify the LAN type and protocol to be used. Where a choice of LAN has to be made, the user is advised to specify a type complying with national or international standards.

(g) **Parallel communications**

Fast or multiplexed communications are sometimes achieved by employing parallel bus techniques. If the user anticipates this form of communication, he would be advised to consider specifying a widely accepted standard or a proprietary standard of a reputable supplier. Non-standard interfaces should be avoided wherever possible, unless the equipment to which the proposed system must interface demands it.

All parallel interface standards (e.g. IEEE 488) impose restrictions on connectors, cable types, cable length, environmental noise (electrical) and number of communicating nodes. The user should, therefore, consider these limits carefully against his requirements, or specify his own requirements clearly to the supplier so that a suitable method may be identified. This is particularly important where coupling to existing or specified interface equipment is involved.

3.3.4 System environment

System environmental factors fall under the headings of **Plant layout**, **Environmental requirements** and **Service capabilities.**

Plant layout

Describe the physical location and arrangement of the plant, indicating all input and output interfaces. Many types of interface have restricted distance capabilities, with associated speed/distance cost trade-offs. The physical layout of plant and computer equipment can have a major effect on the interface requirements and cost.

Environmental requirements

Describe the environment(s) in which the system may have to operate and give details of any standards which may have to be met.

Specify maximum weights and sizes, storage and transportability requirements, colour and styling, noise levels, etc.

(a) **Environmental conditions**

Whilst electronic systems will tolerate a wide variety of environmental conditions, magnetic tapes, magnetic discs and optical discs are susceptible to damage by airborne dirt, dust, mechanical shock or vibration. Magnetic media also require a tighter tolerance on temperature and humidity than electronics.

Any component with moving parts, from cooling fans to printers, will generally require a clean atmosphere and moderate temperature range for trouble-free operation. Chemical contaminants in the atmosphere can damage both electronic and mechanical components. Many system components are affected by magnetic fields, by electrical noise (both mains-borne and radiated), and by RF broadcasts from a close-range source such as a personal radio-phone.

Wherever extremes of temperature, humidity, vibration, magnetic fields, electrical noise or contaminants exist, the user should attempt to reduce the risk. Otherwise the environment should be fully specified to ensure that suitably modified or protected equipment is supplied.

(b) **Health and safety requirements**

In some situations and industries, the environment has to be protected from the equipment in order to meet health and safety requirements, for example in:

> Medical applications
>
> Food processing
>
> Mining and petrochemical industries.

If certain materials are not to be used because they may be hazardous in a given environment, this should be stated.

(c) **Noise control**

Requirements for audible noise control are becoming more onerous, even for office-type equipment, and are increasingly being supported by legislation in European countries. Printers and cooling fans are the worst offenders.

Service capabilities

Specify all available relevant services. This will allow the supplier to design his equipment to suit them or to request additional capabilities. Typically the following information will be required.

(a) **Electrical power.** The availability of 3-phase and single-phase supplies, nominal voltages and frequencies with stability and tolerance figures, maximum load capabilities. Back-up power requirements should also be considered. Also include earthing characteristics.

(b) **Heat removal.** Rated as kW/hour removal rate.

(c) **Compressed air.** Normal pressure and maximum flow rate.

(d) **Mechanical handling.** Fork lift and crane facilities.

Invite the supplier to specify any development facilities he may require during the installation and commissioning period, e.g. special test equipment, additional services, plant availability for hot trials.

3.3.5 System attributes System attributes fall under the headings of **Availability, Maintainability, Adaptability and enhancement potential, Training** and **Documentation.**

Availability

Define the requirements for:

System availability

Recovery from failure.

These will allow the supplier to make proposals for achieving the necessary system integrity by the application of redundancy, error correction or other fault tolerance techniques.

Maintainability

(a) **Diagnostic methods.** Describe any preferred diagnostic methods or procedures for checking and trouble-shooting software-based operational systems. This will enable the supplier to incorporate them into the design proposal where applicable.

(b) **Maintenance support.** State the minimum maintenance support to be provided by the supplier or his agent(s), e.g. 24-hour, seven days a week, with four-hour response.

(c) **Support period.** State the expected design life and required period for spares availability.

Adaptability and enhancement potential

Specify in broad terms any additional functions that may be considered in the future, or any plans for phased implementation of additional facilities.

Most systems will, in time, require extension or modification as demands on the system grow or change. Failure to make due allowance for such change may lead to costly replacement of the system at an early stage in its life. Any statements in the User Requirements Specification concerning the type of development or change that might be anticipated will, therefore, assist the supplier in optimising design decisions, so as not to preclude likely design changes.

Training

Specify training requirements for:

Management

Technical personnel

Operational personnel

Maintenance personnel.

Documentation

(a) **Required documents.** Specify all documents required during the specification, design, development and test stages of the project, and relate their availability to project milestones. Specify all post-installation documentation, with required availability dates. This documentation will include drawings, commissioning and calibration reports, certificates, operating and maintenance information and software descriptions (see Section 7). Define any special requirements such as the supply of documentation in machine readable form. See Section 8.

(b) **Documentation management.** The user is advised to require evidence of satisfactory documentation control procedures on the part of the supplier. The review and approval procedures for all documentation should also be specified. See Section 8.

The user should be aware that in some cases periodic review of the project documentation is the only practical method of assessing the build state of the software and of measuring progress in the development of the system. Professional software skills and knowledge are likely to be required for such reviews and assessment, and so the user may wish to consider the employment of a third party (such as a consultant) for this purpose.

3.3.6 Design, development and test considerations

Design and development requirements

The user may wish to specify the use of a particular programming language or design method, or the use of a particular range of hardware components.

The imposition of such constraints on the supplier may result in a hybrid system with compatibility problems or increased software development and system hardware costs. As a result, any such restrictions on design freedom must be reviewed with the supplier to achieve an optimal solution.

Development requirements

Any requirements imposed on the design and development process by specifying quality assurance and progress reporting procedures, the use of Computer Aided Software Engineering (CASE) tools, phased development and approval stages or documentation standards should be covered in the contractual documentation.

Changes

Formal procedures for making changes to the User Requirements Specification and Functional Specification should be defined (see Sections 8 and 9). Such procedures must be invoked by:

> **The supplier** where, in the course of the project, he anticipates a deviation from or non-compliance with the User Requirements Specification or Functional Specification

> **The user** where his requirements have changed.

The change procedures should include:

> The method by which one party notifies the other of proposed changes

> The method of acceptance or approval of the proposed changes

> The method of incorporating the changes into the documentation.

Quite apart from the technical problems that can arise from late changes, the user should be aware of effects of a commercial nature that can result. Changes should be considered in terms of their effect on

> The functionality of the whole system

> Project timescales

> Project cost.

Testing requirements

Specify all requirements for system simulation, demonstration and acceptance testing (see Section 6).

Testability of the software product is an important consideration not only for system acceptance purposes but also in respect of functional requirements relating to operational objectives and for software development purposes. System hardware maintenance may also be regarded as a key area which will benefit from careful specification of testability in the software.

For further guidance on this topic, the reader is recommended to refer to the IEE publication *Guidelines for assuring testability* which deals comprehensively with the specification and design of testable software. The following extract from that document is reproduced here because of its particular relevance:

> The European Commission Directive on product liability (85/374/EEC) was adopted on 25 July 1985 after some nine years of discussion. The Directive has been implemented in the UK by Part I of the Consumer Protection Act 1987, which came into force on 1 March 1988. This imposes strict liability on the producer for personal injury and damage to private property which arises from a defective product, irrespective of any fault or negligence on the part of the producer.
>
> The advent of strict product liability legislation in the USA has, in recent years, caused designers and manufacturers there to give urgent attention to the adequate testing of their products, particularly in view of the heavy penalties which have been awarded in the Courts when judgements have been made against manufacturers of defective products.
>
> It is not expected that the application of the Consumer Protection Act in the UK will lead to the excessive levels of damages and the associated escalation in insurance premiums seen in the USA. This is partly because damages in the UK are set by a judge rather than by a jury and partly because there is no "contingency fee" system of payment to lawyers such as has led to widespread aggressive litigations in the USA. However, it will be clearly in the interests of producers to ensure that their products are thoroughly tested. Products can only be thoroughly tested if they are designed to be testable—that is the message of these guidelines. Moreover, **complete documentation of the testing strategy, testability reviews and test results needs to be maintained and archived for the life of the product, in case it needs to be produced as evidence.**

Statutory obligations

Ensure that the supplier is aware of his obligations to meet any statutory requirements, such as Health and Safety at Work requirements or audit requirements. Such obligations may apply both during system design and development and during system installation and commissioning.

Specify any local, company or site regulations of a general nature.

3.3.7 Commercial considerations

Acceptable cost

The normal practice will be to invite competitive tenders for the supply of a system to meet the User Requirements Specification. However, in some circumstances it may be desirable to state a target price or price limit.

Timescales

The user should indicate the required date for the availability of the proven system, and may consider making provision in the commercial arrangements for compensation for late delivery. It should be noted, however, that such penalty clauses can be difficult to implement and should not be used as a safety net to guard against an inadequate specification of requirements. The objective of both user and supplier should be to implement a successful system on time.

For a larger project, completion may be specified in well-defined phases, each being covered by some formal assessment of capability. Any preference for project progress-monitoring techniques should be stated.

Other contractual points

Any legal issues concerning ownership, copyright or patent rights to software and its documentation should be addressed in this part of the User Requirements Specification.

For example, the user should seek clarification from the supplier on the ownership of any software to be provided. Where the software runs on a number of systems as well as on the one being purchased, all rights will normally belong to the developer of the software. In cases where software is specially developed for the project, the user's and the supplier's rights to copy and modify the software should be established: the effect of any user modification on the supplier's guarantee should also be clarified.

It is normal practice for suppliers to retain in archive the source material for generating software and its documentation. It may be stored as transparencies, original typescript or in some machine-readable form. The user should specify the minimum period for which the supplier must retain such source material and should also declare his requirement for rights of access to it and authority to copy or reproduce it.

All contractual requirements should be stated, including references and issue numbers of all contract documents.

Provision should be made in the User Requirement Specification for a conformance statement against each of its paragraphs (e.g. by conformance/non-conformance columns).

Section Four: Functional Specification

4.1 Purpose of the Functional Specification

The Functional Specification is usually prepared by the supplier and agreed jointly by supplier and user. It details the manner in which the supplier intends to provide a system to meet the user's needs as set out in the User Requirements Specification. Once agreed by the supplier and the user, it forms part of the contractual documentation, although this approval should not be seen to relieve the supplier of his obligation to provide goods and services in accordance with the contract.

Users should be aware of the contractual conditions offered by the supplier, particularly in respect of the onus of ensuring the extent to which the system offered meets the User Requirement Specification. Any deviations or non-compliance should be resolved prior to placing any contract.

From the user's point of view, the Functional Specification describes what the system will do, how it will be operated and maintained and what facilities will be provided. From the designer's point of view, it provides a list of design objectives and acts as the baseline document for the functions and extent of the proposed system.

Besides covering all system functions, the Functional Specification should, as far as possible, define the attributes of the proposed system. Attributes to be considered include reliability, maintainability, adaptability, ease of training and operation, security and overall quality policy.

Early issues of the Functional Specification are likely to be incomplete, but will form a basis for further discussion and negotiation between user and supplier up to a mutually agreed specification freeze date. During this negotiation period, ambiguities and misunderstandings should be resolved, errors and omissions corrected, and agreement reached on any differences between the tendered solution and the user's stated requirements. It is important that users are made fully aware of the significance of seemingly minor non-compliances which may, nevertheless, unduly restrict the future development of the system software. Omissions and misinterpretations, if not detected at this stage, will inevitably lead to the need for later modifications, with the possibility of delayed operational introduction and increased costs.

Any divergence between the Functional Specification and the User Requirements Specification should be identified by the supplier and clearly documented, giving reasons for the difference. The user should check the Functional Specification for conformance with the User Requirements Specification and resolve any differences. Equally, if deficiencies in the User Requirements Specification come to light or misunderstandings arise in the supplier's interpretation of it, the issues should be resolved and the Functional Specification amended to reflect the new understanding.

In response to some requirements, a supplier may offer an alternative or competitive design which appears almost to comply but at a substantially reduced cost. The issue may be one of performance, but is more likely to be concerned with adaptability, ease of operation or maintenance, or documentation quality. In such cases, the user should estimate the total life cycle costs of the alternative solutions before making a choice.

Because of the contractual nature of the agreed Functional Specification, it should be approved and signed by the user and supplier. Once it has been agreed, the user must ensure that it is kept under formal change control by the supplier to cover any subsequent amendments. Change control should also be applied to any dependent documents. See Section 7.

4.1.1 Scope of the Guidelines

Although the complete Functional Specification will cover both system hardware and system software, the aim of the guidance given here is to ensure that no important software aspects are overlooked.

4.2 Application to different types of system

4.2.1 Fixed program system

For fixed program systems, the supplier's technical specification and users' guide will normally be sufficient to act as the Functional Specification. However, where a considerable investment is contemplated (large numbers of identical systems or high-cost systems), the user may consider it justified to order documentation produced specifically for his application.

4.2.2 Limited variability system

The supplier of a limited variability system should provide a comprehensive standard specification defining each of the basic functional blocks and the method of configuring them into a system. In addition, a formal specification covering the same topics as for a full variability system is strongly recommended (see *4.3* below).

The adaptability and enhancement capabilities of the proposed system should be carefully considered at the Functional Specification stage.

4.2.3 Full variability system

As a full variability system is likely to be tailored for a specific application, an unambiguous and complete Functional Specification is essential.

Any stated or noted divergence from the requirements specified in the User Requirements Specification will need careful consideration by the user prior to agreement.

4.3 Structure of the Functional Specification

As far as possible, the structure adopted for the Functional Specification should parallel that of the User Requirements Specification, to facilitate cross-checking of the two documents. A cross reference should be included in the Functional Specification or other contractual documents, indicating the degree of compliance with the User Requirements Specification.

The following structure is suggested for the Functional Specification:

System overview—providing an overall plan of the supplier's proposed solution. This may take the form of a functional block diagram accompanied by descriptive test (see *4.3.1* below).

Functions to be performed—describing all the functions proposed to meet the system objectives as specified in the User Requirements Specification (see *4.3.2* below).

Application data to be stored—describing all forms of application data stored within the system (see *4.3.3* below).

Facilities to be provided—describing the operational facilities proposed to meet the system objectives as specified in the User Requirements Specification (see *4.3.4* below).

External interfaces—specifying all inputs and outputs of the system, including communication links (see *4.3.5* below).

Attributes—specifying matters relating to the adaptability, availability, maintainability and usability of the system (see *4.3.6* below).

Design, development and test factors—specifying aspects of software design, development procedures and system acceptance testing (see *4.3.7* below).

4.3.1 System overview

The overall description of the proposed solution may take the form of a functional block diagram, i.e. a diagrammatic representation of the essential functions of the system. It should show the relationship between inputs, processes, data storage and output.

Each block in the diagram should represent a clearly defined function or sequence of functions, with defined interfaces to other blocks, plant or associated systems. Secondary systems, such as alarms, diagnostics, training and maintenance aids, should be included. Each block should cross-refer to the full description of the function, interface specification and data flow given elsewhere in the Functional Specification.

For complex systems, a set of diagrams should be produced. In addition to the overall diagram, separate diagrams should be produced for major subsystems and for each individual function and facility.

4.3.2 Functions to be performed

This section of the Functional Specification defines the required functions of the system. The description should be written from the user's viewpoint, but should provide sufficient detail to enable the design to proceed.

The specific objectives of each function should be stated unambiguously. Where possible, the required performance should be defined in measurable terms.

Specify performance objectives and all technical algorithms, formulae and data manipulations for each subsystem or functional block. Include all conditions and exceptions, and all sequential or alternative modes.

The following are typical functions for consideration:

(a) **Normal functions**

Operational Functions

Storage and analysis of historical data

Self-optimising routines

Inter-processor communications (for multi-processor systems)

Synchronisation and flow of control

Control algorithms and models

Start-up and shut-down

Alarm system functions (range limits, rate of change, open circuit, alarm suppression facilities, etc.)

Alarm and failure analysis

(b) **System malfunction and maintenance**

Failure modes and degraded operations

Symptoms and consequences of failure

Error isolation and corrections

Self-checking test programs

Diagnostic routines

Fault routines

Emergency operations.

For each function, performance objectives should be accompanied by limitations or guarantees covering topics such as:

Accuracy

Resolution

Throughput

Response time

Quality

Manpower resource (e.g. operator interaction, maintenance).

4.3.3 Application data to be stored

Describe all forms of application data stored within the system. These will include such things as:

Operational data

Recipes (ingredients, quantities, times)

Look-up tables (including range and resolution inside and outside operating margins: linear or polynomial interpolation)

Conversion tables (e.g. linearisation formulae)

List of coded items

Standard messages

Parameter range limits

Performance limits

Production schedules

Historical operational data (performance and alarm data: event log).

Provide the following information for each item, as appropriate:

Type of storage

Location and extent

Availability

Origin

Responsibility for provision

Access time

Access procedure

Response time

Retention period

Accuracy and resolution

Coding

Updating procedure

Archiving requirements and procedure.

4.3.4 Facilities to be provided

Describe the operational facilities of the proposed system under the headings of **Control and supervision, Safety** and **Security**.

(a) **Control and supervision**

Specify in detail all input and output facilities provided for control, monitoring, scheduling and supervisory operations. Coverage should include specification of:

(i) **Equipment,** for example:

Inputs. Switches, push buttons, keyboard, light pen, joystick, security card reader, magnetic media, voice, digitisers, OCR, optical scanners.

Outputs. Visual display units, mimic diagrams, annunciator panels, lights, meters, bells, buzzers, voice, printers, magnetic media, autodiallers.

(ii) **Operational procedures,** for example,

Operator commands, responses and response times (e.g. for requesting data, calling up alternative displays)

Unsolicited events (e.g. alarms, periodic log outputs, end of batch indication); required response

Override auto-control

Process monitoring

Parameter modifications

Load scheduling

Change of control sequence

System initialisation and shut-down (e.g. program loading and dumping)

Plant start-up and shut-down

On-line routine servicing (e.g. paper and disc replacement, data dumping)

Access security

Emergency procedures

Recovery from operator error

Operator help routines

Operator event logging

(b) **Safety**

Define measures taken to meet any special safety requirements for plant or personnel, with acceptable probabilities of success. Topics to consider include:

Effective software system validation

Rigorous control of changes (see Section 9)

Validation of control inputs and outputs

Safe states on failure

High-integrity alarm systems and interlocks

Containment of errors

Protection of the database from corruption (e.g. duplicate records, periodic on-line validity and integrity checks)

Redundancy

Time-out for operator sign-on

Correct sequencing of operations

Graceful degradation philosophy

Watchdog timer operation

Compliance with Health and Safety at Work and Factory Act legislation

Compliance with safety-related software standards, where appropriate (e.g. HES PES Guidelines, DEF STAN 0055)

Compliance with internal company safety standards.

(c) **Security**

Consider topics as listed for safety above, together with

Restriction of unauthorised access

Data security under fault, misuse and maintenance conditions

Data recovery procedures

Logging and archiving of historical data.

4.3.5 External interfaces

This section defines the detail of all system interfaces with operators, users, plant and communication links. The details should be presented using naming conventions that are applicable to the interface type. Sufficient detail must be given to identify each interface uniquely and to make it clear what the interfaces are and what essential data is passed or needed for control purposes.

(a) **Human interfaces**

(i) **Input**

Define any data to be input to the system by operators, and the manner of input (e.g. menus, soft keys).

(ii) **Output**

Specify the format and content of information output by the system to operators:

Operator supervisor displays, and the manner of presentation

Failure mode information

Alarm signals, and the way in which these are to be presented, acknowledged and accepted

Logging information

Hard copy output

Auto diallers.

Specify the sequence of events and any restrictions on the speed of the operator response.

(b) **Plant/system interfaces**

Give a full specification of the data that will pass at each interface, covering data inputs, telemetry and communication links.

(i) **Inputs**

For each **external input** to the system specify:

Title, reference identity and description, including physical location and address

Source of the input and the nature of the information transferred

Type and format of the input, e.g. analogue, digital, pulse, serial, parallel, binary coded decimal, Gray code

Accuracy and resolution

Range, e.g. 0-500°C, 0-5mA

Interrupts

Default values, for insertion when the input is out of range

Timing, including duration of signal, pulse frequency, minimum and maximum acceptable sampling rates and any synchronization relative to other inputs.

For each **system-derived input** specify:

Title, reference identity and description

Source and nature of the information

Derivation algorithm

Format

Accuracy and resolution

Frequency of calculation

Range

Default values.

(ii) **Outputs**

Specify as for (b)(i) above

Specify the sequence of events and any restrictions on the speed of any required response.

4-7

(iii) **Communications links**

Fully specify any links carrying data into or out of the system. Topics for consideration include:

> Title and description, including standards conformance
> Source or destination of data
> Nature of information to be transferred
> Type of data link (including data rate and timing)
> Protocol (including error checking and retry procedure)
> Polling
> Traffic density and response
> Encryption
> Standards.

4.3.6 System attributes

System attributes are factors relating to the ease and cost-effectiveness of operation, maintenance and extension of the proposed system.

(a) **Availability**

Define the measures to be taken to achieve the required level of system availability. State the Mean-Time-Between-Failure (MTBF) predicted for the system and the method to be used for its verification.

Describe measures to be taken to improve availability (redundancy, error checking, error correction, back-up or stand-by, rejection of human errors, etc.).

(b) **Maintainability**

Cover all provisions made in the design to ensure that the required levels of availability and maintainability are achieved. Include:

(i) **System maintenance philosophy**

> On-line or off-line maintenance facilities
> Built-in diagnostic routines or add-on test equipment.

(ii) **Maintenance facilities and procedures**

> Procedure for reporting and correcting faults after delivery
> Accessibility
> Preventive maintenance schedules and effectiveness
> Structured fault analysis routines
> Fault traceability to lowest replaceable units
> Resident test and diagnostic software
> Plant state diagnosis and prognosis
> Sampled and statistical outputs
> Procedure for testing, integrating and issuing upgraded modules.

(iii) **Resource requirements**

> Test and simulation equipment
> Test software
> Software tools
> Manpower
> Spares holding
> Access to development equipment (when substantial upgrades are required).

(iv) **Effectiveness**

Mean time to:

Locate the error

Repair or replace

Revalidate

Restart.

Possibilities for **degraded operation** during fault conditions:

Criteria allowing various modes of degraded operation

Step-by-step procedures

Recovery procedures back to full operation.

(v) **Support facilities**

Availability of engineering services, with options and costs

Field service call-out procedure

Maintenance facilities

Phone-in query answering service

Spares supply.

(c) **Adaptability and enhancement potential**

Describe in detail the facilities, capabilities and limits within which the system can be adapted or extended.

Adaptability will include ease of tuning for a variable demand and facility for incorporating foreseeable functional and performance extensions.

Areas for concern include:

Connectability, e.g. spare interfaces

Ease of reprogramming or exchanging software modules

Future enhancement and upgrading, including storage expansion

Reduction of human intervention by increase in automatic features

Increased speed of operation

Increased throughput

Extended range of facilities.

(d) **Installation**

Describe the procedures to be applied during the installation of the system, giving attention to:

Transport mechanism to be used

Physical installation of new hardware

Connections to other existing systems

Any required rearrangement of existing plant or equipment

Any required reconfiguration of existing software

Data input/conversion

(e) **Training**

As systems in general become more automatic and more reliable, training methods need to be developed.

When faults rarely occur, initial training is easily forgotten and frequent refresher courses may be essential. An on-line help facility may be a cost-effective way of providing support for the system operation. Methods of simulating or triggering plant failure modes to provide sufficient practice must be considered. This applies to operators, supervisors and maintenance personnel.

Consider the following topics:

(i) **On-line training.** The availability of on-line training using built-in simulators, with plant operational or non-operational.

(ii) **Off-line training.** The provision of off-line training simulators.

(iii) **Structured software.** The provision of structured software systems to minimise requirements for personnel skill and judgement.

(iv) **Documentation.** The provision of high quality documentation for training and operations, giving explicit and easy to understand step-by-step procedures, with explanatory diagrams, and examples.

(f) **Documentation**

Specify all documentation to be supplied to the user during the development and testing stages of the project, with agreed procedures for review and approval. The required availability dates should be clearly stated.

Specify all post-installation documentation to be handed over by the supplier before completion of the contract (see Section 7).

4.3.7 Design, development and test factors

(a) **Design factors**

Describe any special factors relating to the design of the software system. In particular, describe any standard software packages to be used in the system, covering:

Facilities provided

Language

Tailoring requirements

Maintenance and support.

(b) **Development factors**

(i) **Project control**

Outline the methods and procedures to be used by the supplier to monitor and control progress on the project:

Planning and review procedures. Indicate the points in the project life cycle at which major reviews will be carried out. State the criteria for successful achievement of all major milestones.

Quality requirements. Outline the supplier's product assurance philosophy and define its status under any quality assurance certification scheme (e.g. BS 5750/ISO 9000 series, AQAP standards) (see Section 10).

For substantial development tasks, provide quality requirements indicating:

Standards to be applied at all stages, including project management, documentation, technical and administrative standards.

Quality control to be exercised (design reviews, walk-through).

Test and integration procedures for modules.

Configuration management including documentation control, software control, discrepancy reporting and corrective action.

Test and validation procedures for the system.

(ii) **Resource requirements**

Specify what the supplier will require from the user in terms of access, facilities, functions and services during the design, development, installation, testing and in-service support stages of the project.

Access. Supplier staff may require access and accommodation for plant inspection and measurement during the design phase, as well as during installation and testing.

Facilities. Requirements may involve physical plant rearrangement, additional or modified services (e.g. power, heat, light, refrigeration), communications links or off-line computing facilities.

Functions. Modifications to existing plant instrumentation may be needed.

Personnel. Requirements on the user to supply personnel during the installation, testing and in-service support stages should be defined in terms of numbers and skill levels.

Consumables. Examples are paper, magnetic media, spares.

(c) **Test factors**

Specify factors relating to system acceptance testing. System acceptance testing is the method of demonstration by the supplier, witnessed by the user, that the system meets all the contractually agreed requirements.

Include details of

(i) The schedule of tests to be carried out at the supplier's premises before delivery, including any plant simulation

(ii) The schedule of tests to be carried out on site. This may include off-line testing, with or without plant simulation, prior to full on-line testing.

See Section 6 for a full discussion of this topic.

Section Five: Software System Specification

5.1 Purpose of the Software System Specification

The Software System Specification consists of a set of documentation which describes the functions, structure and content of the software system. The specification is produced by the supplier.

Work on this documentation begins once the Functional Specification has been agreed, and continues until the software is tested, accepted and working. In its initial form the specification consists of a detailed statement of design intent. In its final form it constitutes a complete description of the operational software system. At all times, any changes to the software will require a corresponding change to this documentation.

The Software System Specification has two distinct uses:

(a) **Development documentation.** It is used by the supplier's personnel as working documentation during the design and development of the system. During this time, its purpose is to ensure efficient and effective software development.

(b) **Support documentation.** It is used after installation as support documentation, by those responsible for the maintenance and development of the installed system. At this stage, its purpose is to provide enough information to make the software system intelligible to and modifiable by programmers other than those who originally developed the software.

Because of the technical content of the Software System Specification it may be fully intelligible only to people with programming expertise. The user will therefore need to consider his role with regard to this documentation in the light of his requirements and the expertise available to him. Where he has the expertise, he may wish to comment on and/or approve the content of the documentation. Alternatively, he may wish simply to monitor the production of the constituent documentation as a means of checking that the software development is being controlled and progressed according to an agreed plan.

The user should also be aware that he may not be allowed full access to software specifications and source codes where the supplier's proprietary interests are involved (typically for standard software). In such circumstances the user may arrange with the supplier to have the information lodged with a third party and updated as necessary, so that his commercial interests are protected.

The precise extent of the user's access to and role with regard to the Software System Specification must, of course, be agreed with the supplier as part of the contract.

The user must ensure that there is an agreed procedure for identifying and notifying any discrepancies that may arise between the software system as it is developed and the agreed requirements as stated in the Functional Specification. In particular, any divergence caused by an inability fully to meet those requirements must be notified, with detailed reasons for the non-compliance. If after discussion between the supplier and the user it is confirmed that the design is unable to meet the full requirements and an acceptable revision of requirements can be agreed, the Functional Specification should be amended accordingly. Any major problems of this kind may require re-negotiation of the contract.

A variety of descriptive techniques may be used within the Software System Specification, as appropriate to the type of program and software methodology and techniques available. In addition to the descriptive text and source code comment (natural language descriptions), the documentation may include such things as:

Formal language descriptions

Structure diagrams

Data flow diagrams

Decision tables

Other diagrammatic or tabular logical flow representations

Database descriptions including, where appropriate, relational database descriptions, organisation descriptions and file structures.

5.2 Application to different types of system

5.2.1 Fixed program system

The software in an FPS provides a fixed range of functions. A detailed knowledge of the software is normally restricted to the supplier, who has responsibility for it. The supplier's proprietary interests will often result in full details of the software being withheld. However, the user may require such information in certain special cases, e.g. for satisfying the Factory Inspectorate that safety requirements are complied with.

The user should ensure that the supplier provides sufficient information for a precise understanding of what the system does in response to any given set of input data (or information).

5.2.2 Limited variability system

The software in an LVS can be divided into two main categories, **environment software** and **application software.**

Environment software

The environment software is the software which controls and provides computer services for the application software. It may include any software necessary for:

Controlling and allocating the resources of the processors

Providing software development tools, including languages and translators

Driving peripherals

Providing file handling systems, including disk operating systems

Providing user-invisible or transparent functions

Monitoring system integrity

Interpreting the application or command language.

The user will not normally be allowed to develop this software, and so he will only require the information necessary to understand its correct functioning. Full information will be kept by the supplier, but he may limit access by the user to protect his proprietary interests.

Application software

The application software is the software which, together with the environment software, provides a solution to an application problem, i.e. which implements the Functional Specification. In some circumstances it may be developed, amended or extended by the user. Where this is likely to be the case, the user will require detailed system and program specifications, including those covering testing and maintenance. He will also require details of the language(s) in which the software is written.

5.2.3 Full variability system

An FVS will normally be unique for a specific application and will be produced on a one-off or low volume basis. Consequently, except for documentation for the environment software and programming language(s), all software documentation will be specific to the application. The full extent of the documentation should be as described in 5.3 below.

The user should bear in mind that, as with an LVS, the supplier may not allow access to the full environment software documentation, in order to protect his proprietary interests. Users may consider it important to obtain supplier agreement that this documentation be lodged with a third party in order to provide commercial protection.

5.3 Structure of the Software System Specification

The first document to be written for the Software System Specification should be an overall design document specifying:

> **System structure.** The structure of the proposed software system and its breakdown into subsystems.

> **Subsystem structure.** The breakdown of the subsystems into programs and program modules.

> **Data.** Data input to and output from the system.

> **Functions and relationships.** The functions and interrelationships of the various parts of the system.

From this overall design the detailed design of the component parts can be developed. Only when the detailed design and the corresponding module tests have been specified and approved should work begin on coding the program modules.

It may happen that a supplier will offer existing software developed for a similar application but with either extra or more limited facilities. In such a case, the user should seek to ensure that the supplier understands exactly the acceptable minimum level of service that the software must provide, and gain a written assurance from the supplier that this will be met.

As each program module is coded, a document must be produced which describes the module as implemented. In addition, the code must be well annotated with identifying and elucidating comment. The document and the source code listing together constitute the full description of that program module and form part of the Software System Specification.

The following hierarchical structure is recommended for the Software System Specification:

Overall system description

Subsystem descriptions

Program descriptions

Database description.

Where integrated software development and support environments are used in the design, there should be a formal correspondence between each level of documentation in the hierarchy.

The software system should constitute a realisation of the agreed Functional Specification. Cross-references should be given throughout the Software System Specification to those parts of the Functional Specification that are addressed by each software unit.

All documents in the Software System Specification must be kept up to date throughout the software development process. This is to ensure that in its final form the specification is an accurate description of the software system as supplied to the user.

The description of the content of the Software System Specification given in the ensuing sections of the Guidelines is written in terms of the final specification. It does not attempt to define the content of the constituent documents at each stage of the development process; this will vary from supplier to supplier.

5.3.1 Overall system description

The overall system description should include the following information:

System structure

Subsystem and interfaces

Communications between subsystems

Software performance

Input

Output

Security and protection

Recovery from failure

Data amendment facilities

Hardware configuration constraints

Software configuration constraints

Measures for correct operation.

System structure

Identify the logical structure of the complete system and describe how the system has been implemented as a physical structure on a computer.

Specify which structuring methods have been used and state the rationale behind the selection of a particular structure. Document all principal design decisions and identify decisions affecting or having consequences for other system parts. Describe clearly the structure and components of the software and the relationships between them.

Identify those parts of the software system retained in immediate access memory for efficient running, and those parts which are overlaid. Describe implementation features included for the efficient or safe use of memory.

Subsystems and interfaces

Define each subsystem uniquely and define its interfaces to other systems. When standard interfaces are defined and used, fully document any exceptions, giving reasons for the exceptions.

Show the inter-relationships between all the subsystems of the system.

Communications between subsystems

Identify all communications channels between subsystems. Describe modes of access, communications protocol, channel capacity, throughput, or throughput delay. Include a statement of any synchronisation, performance or safety-related features of the communications channels.

Identify any facilities provided to enable the user to communicate with either systems or computer networks to provide or acquire data for associated tasks.

Software performance

Describe the scheduling of the system, including the latest times at which input data will be available and at which output data can be computed. Include response times or elapsed times and a description of the actions which the system will take in the event of unavoidable delay.

Give details of throughput times, the response times of major system functions, the priorities in various modes of operation and the priorities imposed by various inputs. Include details of dynamic performance measures taken under various levels of imposed load under different operating modes or conditions.

Input/output

Define the unique correspondence between each external (physical) input or output and the identification of the data as known to the computer system.

(a) **Data input**

For each data input provide the following implementation information:

Identifier (physical) of the external input

Identifier (logical) of the input

Description of the data and brief explanation of its use

Format of the data

Range of data, i.e. the range of values that are valid

Timing information, including latest time at which data may be input to the computer and any synchronization relative to other inputs.

Acceptance tests and description of error detection/error handling

Ability to recreate the data or insert default values in the event of error or failure

Scope of the data (identification of that part of the program in which the data may be used and classification of the type of expression in which it may form a valid argument)

Location of the data (reference to the logical identifier of the file(s) in which the data is stored).

(b) **Interrupt inputs**

If application-related interrupts are allowed in the system, then for each interrupt input provide the following information:

Identifier (physical) of the interrupt

Identifier (logical) of the interrupt

Description of the interrupt and brief explanation of its use

Interrupt usage and masking;

and, in all systems in which interrupts are allowed:

Clear identification of critical sections of the software (in which interrupt handling must be inhibited)

Priority, where appropriate.

(c) **Data output**

For each data output provide the following information:

Identifier (physical) of the external output

Identifier (logical)) of the data output

Description of the data and usage

Format of the data

Range of the data

Ability of the software to produce a well-defined output in the event of error or failure, including details of deterministic output and identification of any indeterminate outputs.

Security and protection

Describe the features included to protect programs and data from

Accidental loss or corruption

Unauthorised access or change

where such events could arise during normal or abnormal operation or during power failures, hardware failures or faults in the software leading to errors or failure.

Describe security aspects: in particular, how memory space for constants and instructions is protected or supervised against change or unauthorised read/write operations.

Identify the extent, if any, to which plant operators are allowed access to data or program code.

Recovery from failure

Give a system-level description of the way in which tasks can be delayed, suspended or terminated. Give details of procedures or automatic means to run down the system (graceful degradation) and to terminate and turn-off the system. Fully document any side effects of the degradation procedures which may have implications for safety or the security of essential data.

Give full details of the method for restoring the capabilities of a degraded system, or for initiating and restarting a system which has been shut down or failed, including all information necessary for the system to be brought into operation in a controlled and safe manner.

Data amendment facilities

Where there is a requirement for data to be changed, there should be a secure but easy-to-use data amendment facility. Describe the facilities provided to allow system-level data to be inspected or modified, both on-line and off-line. Give details of the methods used to limit access to or alteration of data and to introduce new data values or modify existing data.

Hardware minimum and maximum configuration

Identify hardware resource requirements and constraints. Specify the minimum system hardware configuration on which the software supplied will operate to meet the performance criteria given in the Functional Specification.

Identify the extent to which the system hardware can be expanded without effect on the supplied software.

Software minimum configuration

Identify clearly the minimum configuration of software modules consistent with system operation for the duties specified.

This is particularly important when the operating system is formed from a kernel of necessary procedures surrounded by a shell of optional operating system features. Similarly, application software may consist of a set of software procedures augmented by a library of general and specialised software routines which may be configured to specific applications.

Measures for correct operation

Describe the measures taken and/or techniques used to ensure the correct design and operation of the system for the duties for which it is to be applied. This may include details of:

(a) **Structure method.** Describe the method or design approach adopted to ensure a coherent and secure implementation of the system and its software.

(b) **Interrupt or state-driven systems.** Many control, automation, on-line and monitoring systems have state and event-driven software tasks which are activated on the occurrence of a specific event (including external calls, interrupts or real-time clocks). Describe any such systems, their operation, action and side effects, and default actions in the event of illegal calls to the system.

(c) **Concurrency.** Concurrent processes must share system resources or allocate physical resources in a predictable and safe manner. Describe these actions and specify the precautions taken to ensure safe operation in such environments.

(d) **Dynamic performance monitors.** Describe any measures taken to monitor the dynamic behaviour of the system software (e.g. watchdogs or time-out) and its usage of bounded or limited resources. Describe default modes clearly.

5.3.2 Subsystem descriptions

For each subsystem, documentation must be provided that describes its function, operation, inter-connectivity and database usage.

The full documentation of each subsystem will include the following information.

(a) **Functional description.** Details of the work each subsystem is to perform and its relationship to all other subsystems within the overall system.

(b) **Interfaces to other systems or subsystems.** Details of all inter-dependencies between each subsystem and other systems and subsystems.

(c) **Subsystem controls.** A detailed list of those controls or parameters specifically provided by or for each subsystem to ensure its correct setting up, operation and continued integrity.

(d) **Data input, output and associated protocols.** A comprehensive list of all data types used, methods of data input and output and verification. Details of all associated protocols used in the receipt or transmission of data to or from the system.

(e) **Data flow and database usage.** Details of the data entering and leaving each subsystem and common associated database or other global data area.

(f) **Program flow control.** A clear description of any hardware or software used to co-ordinate and schedule program activity or program flow in a controlled manner. Details of any mechanism used to ensure correct running of program sequences.

(g) **Timer scheduling and default action.** The method of initiation and scheduling of start-up or timed entry of programs, including default actions when sequences fail or timings are in error; the response of the system or subsystems to erroneous timing signals, with details of traps or default actions to protect against such mishaps.

(h) **Initialization, restart and recovery procedures.** A detailed description of the procedures for bringing the system and associated subsystems into operation in a controlled and safe manner. A description of the procedure for running down and turning off the system in a manner which will not disrupt the process being controlled or monitored. A description of the restart and recovery procedure after failure or other stoppage.

(i) **Data amendment facilities.** Details of all facilities provided to enable data to be modified, either on-line or off-line, indicating the protection provided to maintain safe and reliable operation of the system.

5.3.3 Program descriptions

Note that the supplier may be prepared to release this information for special-to-project software only.

A description of each program module must be produced, covering the following points:

> The function of the module
>
> Method and, where relevant, periodicity of entry
>
> Reference to all external data structures accessed for this application
>
> All possible outputs
>
> Details of interlocks
>
> Detailed logic and structure of the code
>
> Internal data formats
>
> Intermediate communication within the module.

An annotated listing of the source code should be produced, cross-referenced to its associated descriptive document.

Some languages are considered to be self-documenting and will, for example, provide a pictorial representation of a program. It is important, however, to structure the software in a sensible manner, so that the intended logic can be easily understood and developed. Also, however good a self-documenting system may be, it will invariably require some supplementary information in order to define and describe its functions clearly.

5.3.4 Database description

The system database usually includes all the items of data used by the system for a given application. The majority of these data items emanate from parts of the system and its component subsystems. They are held for use by the system as a whole.

The documentation should provide a comprehensive description of the database provided for this application, including the following:

(a) **File and record structure.** The structure of the data, its position in the database and any relationships with other associated data or data sets.

(b) **Data items.** A detailed list of individual items of data with information on:

> Physical name and identifier
>
> Physical range of variable
>
> Range of logical variable
>
> Upper and lower limits of the data
>
> Format type or encoding (ASCII, BCD, binary, floating point).

The description should indicate whether item values are static or change dynamically under working conditions.

(c) **Relational structure.** The way the data is structurally related, so that areas of items within the database can be located. Describe any specific facilities or access methods used.

(d) **Access protocols.** Details of any protocols used to access or control access to the database or to encode or segregate items.

(e) **Access protection.** Methods used to restrict unauthorised access to the system (e.g. write protect), together with details of any synchronisation techniques. Describe the method of removing protection to allow and control amendment.

(f) **Method of construction and amendment.** The mechanism for constructing the database, with details of all facilities built into the system to enable the user to add, delete or amend any data item in the database.

(g) **Storage media.** The type, size and expandability of the database storage medium (main store, disk, etc.). Include information on redundant copies of data held on backing store and the procedure for updating them and archiving data for long term record keeping.

Section Six: System Acceptance Testing

6.1 Purpose of System Acceptance Testing

System acceptance testing is the means by which the supplier demonstrates to the user that the total system requirements, as embodied in the agreed Functional Specification, have been met. The tests are carried out by the supplier and are witnessed by the user.

Testing will in most cases be carried out in two stages: **before delivery,** on the supplier's premises, and **after installation,** on the user's site. Testing may be further sub-divided if a phased sequence of delivery and system build-up is planned.

Conditions which are to be satisfied before the start of acceptance testing should be stated in the User Requirements Specification and included in the Test Plan. It is suggested that such conditions should include some assurance that all designated hardware and software is available and has been tested to the supplier's satisfaction and that all post-installation documentation is available.

Subject to the terms of the contract, satisfactory completion of the acceptance tests will lead to:

Formal acceptance of the system

Payment by the user

Handover of all deliverables (i.e. possession passes to the user)

Start of the warranty period

Start of any support and maintenance agreements.

The user should set out his requirements for system testing in the User Requirements Specification. Information on how these requirements are to be met should be included in the Functional Specification. It is particularly important that the supplier should produce an overall test philosophy and test plan at an early stage in the contract negotiations, and that these should be agreed by the user. The Test Plan details the testing activities and the organisation of those activities which are to be used to establish that the system satisfies the contractual statement of requirements. The remaining test documentation should be produced by the supplier during the development of the system, with all documents being agreed by both parties.

It is the supplier's responsibility to produce the test documentation, which should include:

Test philosophy

Test plan

Test specifications

Test logs

Test summary

Commissioning report

Certificate of acceptance.

6.1.1 Scope of the Guidelines System acceptance testing involves all aspects of the system—hardware, application software, environment software, plant and operators. The Guidelines, therefore, do not attempt to treat software testing separately from the other aspects of system testing.

6.2 Application to different types of system

6.2.1 Fixed program system Assessment of performance of the system against the criteria in the published specification of data sheets is usually sufficient for an FPS. However, suppliers will often publish a test procedure for checking out the system in-situ, and/or on the bench.

Fixed program systems should be self-checking as far as is practicable; certainly the software (which will be held in ROM) should be error-checked periodically.

The user should ensure that sufficient information is available from the supplier to satisfy himself that the system functions correctly.

6.2.2 Limited variability system The two categories of software in an LVS can be considered separately, although it should be noted that environment software and application software will have a close liaison under operational conditions. For example, the application software may require to be advised of an operating system status which will cause it to take appropriate application action. On the other hand, plant conditions may be monitored directly by the environment software to ensure total integrity. A watchdog timer interlock is a typical example of this.

It should be possible for a standard check-out procedure to be obtained for the environment software of an LVS. All that was stated above for fixed program systems is applicable to such software.

In some limited variability systems it is necessary to load application software which will perform the role of a validation procedure (principally for use on the bench). This type of arrangement will also often require a test rig for plant interface simulation. The user should ensure that full documentation for this level of testing is provided.

In addition to the above, the test specifications for the application software should be produced in accordance with the recommendations given in *6.3.3* below.

6.2.3 Full variability system The greater the complexity of the system and the less proven its design, the more likely it is that there will be inherent faults in its design and construction. Thus the tests applied to a complex and important system need to be extremely rigorous and comprehensive. These are likely to be time-consuming and expensive. Yet even the most detailed and prolonged testing cannot prove beyond all doubt that a system is error-free and will remain so. Users are therefore faced with deciding upon the degree of confidence which is acceptable for the application. This must be reflected in the agreed test philosophy, particularly in the inclusion of any requirement for prolonged periods of testing for confidence building. Nevertheless, the responsibility for the production of a system which meets the Functional Specification rests with the supplier.

6.3 Acceptance Testing Documentation and Procedures

The ensuing sections provide some recommendations for consideration when defining the extent of acceptance tests to be undertaken and the detailed content of the test documentation. Advice is also given on procedures to be followed and documentation to be produced during pre-delivery tests and site acceptance tests.

General points for consideration with regard to testing are discussed below.

Hardware testing

It is usual for the hardware to be tested in isolation from the system software before any system acceptance testing is undertaken. However, such tests can only test the hardware to a limited extent. It is important to realise that hardware tests cannot always ensure that the hardware will operate in the same way when under the control of the system software and cannot always be relied upon to show up every hardware fault, whether permanent or intermittent, that may affect the system software.

Software module testing and integration

Some projects may require separate delivery of software or hardware components. In this case, tests for each software module should be individually documented. A final, integrated test procedure is then required to cover the full system, including any separately accepted modules.

Pre-delivery testing

Maximising the extent of pre-delivery testing has the advantage of reducing the risk of serious problems arising during the final acceptance test on site, where it is more difficult, costly and time consuming to rectify faults. Thus, as much testing as possible should be carried out on the supplier's premises where strong technical support and facilities will be at hand to correct any revealed deficiencies. Detail of likely plant operation, data, etc. should be provided by the user to enable the supplier to provide adequate plant simulation equipment for pre-delivery testing. The onus should be placed on the supplier to ensure that the system will pass the pre-delivery tests prior to the formal witnessed tests taking place. This should save time by minimising restarts and retests.

Continuous operation

Since it takes time for some hardware weaknesses to become apparent, it may be considered worthwhile to include periods of continuous operation, both before delivery and on site, before final acceptance. However, special environmental tests to demonstrate operation under extended conditions, either pre-delivery or on site, can be costly. The need for them should, therefore, be judged in relation to the severity of the operational requirements and the projected total life cycle costs. In this context the advantage of using well proven hardware, environment software and application software will be self-evident.

Test Plan

A schedule of test activities should be agreed at the start of the contract: this should form the basis of the Test Plan. Dates should be agreed for the supplier to have access to site for installation and test purposes. Any requirement for special site services, lifting equipment, power supplies, etc. should be determined early in the contract and responsibility agreed.

User involvement

The degree of user involvement in the testing phase of a project is a matter for early agreement with the supplier. Aspects for agreement include:

    User attendance at formal pre-delivery testing

    Conditions to be met before delivery to site

    Criteria for starting tests

    Criteria for abandoning tests

    Procedure for re-running tests

    Procedure for concession of test specification changes.

Premature start of acceptance tests and premature delivery to site can lead to operational delays, loss of confidence by operational and managerial staff, and difficulty in agreeing responsibility for extra costs incurred.

6.3.1 Test philosophy

The objective of the system acceptance tests is to demonstrate to the user, with an acceptable degree of confidence, that the system will meet the requirements of the Functional Specification. This should include all necessary detail to ensure that the system is:

    Operationally safe and secure

    Reliable

    Maintainable in a cost-effective manner

    Modifiable to meet changing operational requirements.

As part of his test philosophy, the supplier should explain in general terms how this objective is to be achieved.

Because it is not possible to test every conceivable combination of circumstances, considerable technical skill is required in the selection and specification of the tests. It is worth noting that tests should be included to check all alarm functions and to check the consequences of incorrect or false data or operating instructions, to ensure that no system mal-operation takes place under such conditions.

Further guidance on testing is contained in the IEE publication *Guidelines for Assuring Testability*.

6.3.2 Test Plan

This document, usually prepared by the supplier and agreed by the user, consists of the schedule of tests to be applied in both pre-delivery and site acceptance trials, together with the procedures to be followed in carrying out the tests.

Contents of a Test Plan

This document should include

(a) **Test philosophy.** The philosophy of testing, indicating the reasoning leading to the choice of tests.

(b) **Test items.** A schedule of all items to be tested and items to be excluded.

(c) **Test sequence.** The sequence of tests to be performed (indicating the relationship and any interdependence between tests) and their individual purpose related clearly to specific requirements of the Functional Specification.

(d) **Test method.** The method of carrying out each test (leaving detailed instructions to be given in the Test Specification, see *6.3.3*).

(e) **Test resources.** The resources required for each test, covering hardware, software, simulation equipment, special test equipment, test data (including timing constraints) and personnel.

(f) **Resource provision.** Defined responsibilities and timing for the provision of the test resources.

The Test Plan should demonstrate compliance with the Functional Specification and include provision for tests to prove that the system will reject false data or instructions and will maintain the safety and security of the system under all possible conditions, and should indicate test specifications and test data.

General test procedures

The Test Plan should specify the overall procedures for setting up and managing the acceptance test operations, and include definitions of the following:

(a) **Supervisor and invigilator.** The appointment by the supplier of a trials supervisor, and by the user of a trials invigilator or approver with authority to sign the test record and approve reasonable variations or deviations from the schedule. This is to ensure that tests are carried out in conformance with agreed procedure, and to enable on-the-spot decisions to be taken in agreeing any necessary schedule changes during the course of the testing.

(b) **Schedules and location.** Procedures and responsibilities for arranging time schedules and place of the tests (with sufficient notice for adequate preparation of all resources) and for specifying and checking the provision and correct supply of all trials requirements.

(c) **Changes to plan.** Procedures to be followed in agreeing tactical changes to the planned sequence of tests ꞏor their detailed specification.

(d) **Test failure.** Procedures to be followed on failure of a test, e.g. the number of retries allowed, agreeing the degree of retesting after modification, etc.

(e) **Test results.** Procedures for documenting, summarising and reviewing the results of the tests.

(f) **Completion criteria.** Definition of criteria for successful completion of pre-delivery test (leading to delivery to site) and site acceptance test (leading to handover of ownership and payment).

6.3.3 Test Specifications

Each test to be applied to the system must be specified by the supplier in complete detail and approved by the user. Failure properly to specify the tests to be carried out, prior to testing, could lead to serious problems later on.

All specifications should, as far as possible, include the following points:

Test title and unique reference

Test objective, specifically related to a requirement of the Functional Specification (reference to the appropriate paragraph should be included)

Location of the test and organisation of the testing activities

Test conditions, e.g. whether marginal values of inputs, supplies and environment are to be used

Test configuration, with required version or issue levels of all hardware, software, test and simulation aids and software tools

Specification for input and output

Detailed operational procedure for carrying out the test

Desired results and acceptable limits, including pass/fail criteria (these may be in the form of numerical data or a checklist of events, messages or graphical information)

Format for recording test results, details of failures and instructions for retest, recording, record retention and analysis.

6.3.4 Pre-delivery tests

The importance of comprehensive pre-delivery testing, with plant equipment simulation where appropriate, has already been emphasised. The following points should be covered during the testing:

Conditions for starting the test

Previously agreed conditions for starting the test must be met or a formal concession granted. This involves checking the availability and correctness of all data, documentation, application software and special test or simulation software, and the availability of an acceptable environment, services and suitable personnel.

Hardware and software build

The build standard or issue levels of all hardware and software to be used in the test should be checked and documented (see Section 9).

Preliminary hardware test

All hardware to be used in the functional testing of the system should be required to pass an agreed preliminary hardware performance acceptance test to ensure known hardware operability before software testing begins.

Test Plan

The agreed Test Plan must be followed (see 6.3.2).

Test Procedures

Agreed Test Procedures must be adhered to (see 6.3.2).

Test Log

A Test Log of all operations and events, planned and unplanned, should be rigorously maintained, including full details of all incidents, operator errors, failures, restarts and retests. All entries should be referenced, to allow cross referencing to items included in the Test Summary.

System diagnostics

The means of fault detection and diagnostics provided by the system software should be validated. This will involve making provision for inducing a sufficient variety of faults and out-of-range conditions in the system to ensure that the detection processes are adequately tested.

Functional testing

Functional testing using the system software should be comprehensive. Simulation of the inputs and responses from plant and operation should be as realistic a reproduction as possible of expected site conditions. Marginal limit values of inputs, supplies and environment should be included in the test conditions.

Test Summary

Following completion of the tests, a Test Summary should be prepared by the supplier, listing all test failures (including repeated tests), unexplained incidents and non-conformances to the Functional Specification. The list should be suitably referenced to provide clarity in the follow-up investigations, discussions and interpretation of test results. Any changes may involve configuration management (see Section 9).

Test failures

The courses of action to resolve failures and problems arising during the tests, as itemised in the Test Summary, should be agreed. The user may agree to accept certain deficiencies or limitations, either permanently or for a specified period of time during which the supplier is required to provide a correction. In other cases the user may need to insist on delaying delivery to site until a deficiency is corrected. Where later modifications are carried out to correct deficiencies, this may invalidate tests already carried out and the extent of system retest will need to be agreed.

Clearance for delivery

The user should not give clearance for delivery to site until he is completely satisfied that the agreed and essential tests have been carried out and any resulting actions agreed. Where the control of an active plant is involved, the user will require to be convinced, before delivery, that the system will be safe and will cause no damage to the plant.

Abandoning tests

The user must assess at what point testing should be abandoned in cases where failures are such that they call into question the basis of continued testing.

6.3.5 Site Acceptance Tests

In considering the final site acceptance testing which precedes system handover, all the points covered in the paragraphs on pre-delivery tests are applicable (see 6.3.4). Additionally, the following aspects require consideration before the final functional proving tests are attempted.

Delivery checks

All delivered hardware, software media and documentation should be checked for damage, completeness, and build and issue level.

Hardware testing

All delivered hardware should be required to pass an agreed level of testing prior to connection to the user's plant, to ensure that it:

(a) Has not suffered any loss of performance due to storage or transit damage

(b) Has been installed correctly

(c) Operates satisfactorily with site electrical supplies in the site environment and performed at the same level as in the pre-delivery tests.

Testing pre-delivery modifications

Any modifications agreed as a consequence of problems arising during pre-delivery testing should be subjected to additional proving tests.

Plant equipment checks

All plant equipment should be checked for conformance to specification and freedom from faults prior to connection to the delivered system.

Support requirements

All specified requirements for accommodation, environment, services and support should be met, or concessions agreed and documented.

The site testing should build up to cover the full extent of the Test Specifications, and should prove as much as possible of the Functional Specification. Initially, the use of some simulation techniques may be necessary, prior to full plant or system operation, particularly if a phased build-up of the system has been planned.

The site test schedule will naturally break down into the following phases:

(a) **Hardware validation testing.** The use of hardware test programs to demonstrate the correct operation of all hardware.

(b) **Hardware testing with site connections.** This may need to follow an incremental build-up to full connection.

(c) **Fault validation testing.** Responses to out-of-limit inputs and induced faults or failures arising in the plant, plant instrumentation or control system should be rigorously checked.

(d) **Functional testing.** Comprehensive system functional testing under all modes of operation, e.g. start-up, manual, automatic, standby, power fail and recovery.

(e) **Extended running.** Extended running, where specified, to demonstrate reliable operation.

Other aspects which should not be overlooked include:

Training of operational staff

Training of maintenance staff

Any requirements for tuning the system, e.g. for maximum throughput, maximum efficiency, minimum cost

Adequate proving of alarm, safety, security and back-up systems.

Following conclusion of the site testing, a **Test Summary** report should be prepared and signed by both parties, to provide the basis for a post-mortem analysis. This may lead to further modification and retesting before a **Certificate of Acceptance** is formally signed by the user.

Finally, a **Commissioning Report** should be provided to give the installed state of the system. This should include a definition of the modification state of both hardware and software (see Section 9).

6.3.6 Takeover and acceptance

The final acceptance of a system may have two stages: **takeover** and **acceptance**. Takeover is the stage at which the user agrees that the *equipment* meets the requirements of the Functional Specification in principle, but requires an agreed period of trouble-free operation as the final demonstration of acceptability. Hardware warranties normally come into effect at takeover. Acceptance is the stage at which the user agrees that the *software* meets his requirements. Software warranties normally come into effect at this point.

The user is advised that a supplier's interpretation of the terms **takeover** and **acceptance** may differ from the above. It is therefore important that the exact definition of these terms is stated in the contract documents. This is particularly advisable in cases where the total system implementation is to be carried out in phases over a period of time.

Section Seven: Post-Installation Documentation

7.1 Purpose of post-installation documentation

The purpose of post-installation documentation is to describe the system as installed and to provide sufficient information for users, maintainers and developers to execute their responsibilities throughout the working life of the system. The documentation generated in the course of the project to communicate design objectives and proposals between the user and the supplier and to disseminate technical information within the supplier's design team will provide sufficient information to satisfy most of these needs, but it may sometimes require to be supplemented with other information or to be presented in a different form appropriate to a changed readership.

It is important to note that although post-installation documentation is intended for use after installation, this does not imply that such documentation is *produced* after installation.

The user is strongly advised to arrange formal assessment and acceptance procedures for post-installation documentation. This should take place at the time of the system acceptance tests when the documentation can most readily be checked for completeness and accuracy. The availability of such documentation should be considered as a prerequisite for the start of acceptance testing.

7.2 Application to different types of system

7.2.1 Fixed program system

With this type of system, the degree of user involvement in fault diagnosis and repair will determine the extent of the documentation that should be provided. Typically, such systems form components of larger systems and responsibility for diagnosis of faults down to major system component level is all that is required of the user, the offending FPS being returned to the manufacturer or his agents for repair.

If repair down to circuit component level is required, circuit diagrams, component lists and service manuals will be needed. This level of documentation would also give some degree of protection against the supplier failing to provide a repair service in the future, and it is therefore sensible to obtain and hold it against such an eventuality. The ability to reproduce the software should also be secured for the same reason. Proprietary interests may demand that such capability be held by an agreed third party, subject to suitable legal arrangements being made.

If the user contemplates maintaining this type of system down to circuit component level, including reproduction of software, he should be aware of any special equipment and specialist technician skills that may be necessary, such as the ability to prepare PROMs from source media.

7.2.2 Limited variability system

For a limited variability system, the comments made in *7.2.1* apply only to the system hardware and the environment software. For application software follow the recommendations given in *7.3* below.

7.2.3 Full variability system

All topics discussed in *7.3* should be considered carefully for full variability systems.

7.3 Requirements for post-installation documentation

The user may prefer to prepare some or all of the post-installation documentation himself, using the project documentation as source information. This may be desirable where, for example, local or internal standards for documentation have to be satisfied. If the supplier is required to prepare this documentation, he should be made aware of this at the user requirements stage of the project, and be advised of the documentation standards (if any) which will apply.

In either case, the supplier should be advised in the User Requirements Specification of all relevant information that must be provided by the end of the project, and formal agreement should be obtained on the responsibility for providing those parts of the post-installation documentation which are to be specially written. If the supplier is required to provide operating procedure manuals, the user will need to make the necessary procedural information available to the supplier on an agreed timescale.

Formal procedures for updating the post-installation documentation should be specified in the User Requirements Specification and agreed by the supplier. The required availability dates for document drafts and updates, related to project milestones, should also be specified in the User Requirements Specification.

As already stated, much of the documentation generated during the course of the project will contain essential information for operating, maintaining and developing the system. It is desirable and cost-effective to arrange for such documentation to address these needs when first generated. The originators of the documents should, therefore, consider their suitability for these purposes.

The following sections list the requirements for post-installation documentation under the headings **General documentation, Operational use, Maintenance** and **Further development of the system**. In the light of the guidance given, the user may decide how comprehensive his post-implementation documentation needs to be, how he wishes it to be presented, and by whom.

7.3.1 General documentation

General documentation will include the following:

Test, commissioning and calibration reports (see *6.3.5*)

Acceptance certificates (see *6.3.5*)

Standards documentation

Drawings

Warranty—conditions, start dates, end dates

Hardware maintenance agreements/contracts

Fault reporting procedures

Post-installation special-to-project software upgrade and enhancement procedures, including documentation updates

Notification procedure and maintenance contracts for supported software updates (e.g. operating system, language compilers)

Transfer of title/ownership of software modules

Permits/certificates authorising the use of licensed or leased software.

7.3.2 Operational use

General description

Operational documentation should include a general description of the facilities available to each operator who will communicate with the system, including those operators who will only receive outputs from the system or be affected in some other way by the system. All controls, screen and printout formats and keyboard layouts should be fully described. All such information should be produced in a form suitable for future reference, e.g. as a training manual.

Messages and alarms

All messages, alarms and indications from the system should be described with respect to:

> Possible cause(s)
>
> Probable consequence(s) if ignored
>
> Recommended operator action.

Operator actions

All prescribed operator control actions, keyboard entry sequences, etc., should be defined in terms of:

> Purpose and reason for the action
>
> Effect or consequence of the action or entry
>
> Any interlocks preventing such action or entry
>
> Ranges and logical checks applied.

External events and conditions

All foreseeable external events and conditions should be defined, together with their consequential effects on the system, e.g. mechanical failure of components of the controlled plant, loss of supply to remote stations, computer room air conditioning failure.

Operational procedures

Using the above information, the user will need to specify the detailed operational procedures his staff are to follow in running the system as part of the overall plant operation.

Presentation

It is important that operational and procedural documentation is presented in an understandable manner for the operator who will use it. Jargon and technical expositions should be avoided. The information should be presented to each operator on a 'need to know' basis.

7.3.3 Maintenance

Information requirements for system maintenance include the following:

(a) **Start-up and shut-down.** System start-up and shut-down procedures.

(b) **Parameters.** Configurable (on-line) system parameters and options; the method by which they may be altered, including guidelines describing the reasons for doing so.

(c) **Environment software regeneration.** Procedures for regeneration of the as-installed environment software from source material, e.g. operating system and language compiler.

(d) **Application software regeneration.** Procedures for regeneration of the application software (including assembly/build time options) from supplied source material or media.

(e) **Security copies.** Procedures for maintaining security back-up copies of environment software, application software, static data files and live data files, and the method of reconstituting these from the back-up copy.

(f) **Utilities.** Operating instructions for all system utility features, e.g. disc formatter/initialiser, crash dump utility analyser.

(g) **Error/log messages.** A comprehensive list of all system error messages and log messages, including cause, consequence and recommended actions on the occurrence of each.

(h) **Fault investigations.** Agreements procedures for escalation of all fault investigations, e.g. will the supplier provide off-site consultancy for suspected application software or standard software problems?

(i) **Diagnostics.** Diagnostic methods and any performance reporting facilities.

7.3.4 Further system development

In most cases this will be the most difficult aspect of post-installation documentation to specify comprehensively. Unless the proposed future developments are clearly and precisely defined, it will not be possible to guarantee the availability of all the information which a future developer of the system may require. Consideration of the following topics, however, should reduce the risk to a minimum.

(a) **Environment software documentation.** Most system designers establish the operating environment of the application software at an early stage in the design, and all subsequent design statements assume a knowledge of that environment. Certain key design features may, therefore, be embedded within the operating environment. Thus it is important to obtain a full description of the operating system and the method by which the application software (current and future) may interface to it and utilise its various features and facilities. Normally such information is provided by standard documentation describing the operating system.

For similar reasons a full set of documentation should be obtained for the language compilers, task builders, linkage editors and all available utilities.

(b) **Operating system modification.** Full instructions for expanding, altering and re-generating the operating system to accommodate software or hardware developments should be obtained. Also the limitations applicable to expansion and/or amendments should be stated. This information will usually be contained in standard documentation.

(c) **Source code listings.** Fully annotated source listings of all software system modules (standard and special-to-project) should be requested. Where the supplier is reluctant to provide such information for reasons of proprietary interest, a suitable alternative arrangement should be agreed, e.g. the holding of the information by a third party.

The annotated listings should be supplemented by descriptive text and relevant diagrams (flow diagrams etc.) such that all software modules are clearly described and that the inter-module interfaces and global references are clearly defined.

(d) **Data structures.** All file structures, internal lists and tables must be comprehensively described.

It will be obvious that most of the above information is provided by the Software System Specification supplemented by standard documentation for the standard software. However, it is in the area of minute and precise detail that system developers may find information lacking. Therefore careful attention to detail is important here if useful documentation is to be provided.

Section Eight: Documentation Management

8.1 Purpose of Documentation Management

The consistent production of good quality software documentation by a supplier is dependent on the way in which documentation is managed. Good management practices help to ensure that documentation is produced

With accurate, complete and unambiguous content

For the people who need it

When it is needed

In the form in which it is needed

At a reasonable cost.

The management practices described in this Section are applicable to the production of documentation for FPSs, LVSs and FVSs. Naturally, the effort involved in the management of documentation will vary according to the size of the company and size and complexity of the software engineering projects undertaken. However, the use of a full documentation management system will result in the efficient production of effective documents and is, therefore, a sensible investment for any company.

8.1.1 Scope of the Guidelines

The Guidelines describe those aspects of documentation management that the user should look for in satisfying himself that a supplier will produce good software documentation.

Section 8.2 indicates the extent to which the user is advised to consider a supplier's documentation management practices for the different types of system.

Good management practices are discussed in Sections 8.3 to 8.8. Section 8.4 deals with the use of documentation standards. Section 8.5 describes documentation procedures. Section 8.6 discusses the application of quality assurance to documentation. The benefits to be gained from using documentation methods, techniques and tools are outlined in Section 8.7. Section 8.8 deals with staffing considerations.

8.2 Application to different types of system

8.2.1 Fixed program system

Effective documentation management is as important for fixed program systems as for any other type of system. However, the user will not normally need to concern himself with the supplier's documentation management practices, since the documentation will already be published and can be directly assessed for quality.

8.2.2 Limited variability system

For limited variability systems most of the documentation will be standard and will be available for inspection before the contract is placed. However, the user may wish to check the supplier's documentation management practices to ensure that the system will be adequately supported after installation.

8.2.3 Full variability system

With full variability systems, much or all of the documentation will be produced after the contract has been signed. In these circumstances it is advisable to check before placing the contract that suppliers manage their documentation effectively, to give confidence that good documentation will be produced for the system.

As part of the tendering process for FVSs, the user is advised to prepare a list of questions relating to documentation management and to ask potential suppliers for written answers.

Particularly where a large or complex system is planned, the user should ensure that the supplier

> Uses documentation standards and procedures (including configuration control and quality control procedures relating to documentation)

> Produces documentation as an integral part of every stage of a project's development

> Subjects documentation to formal review and approval

> Uses appropriate documentation methods, techniques and tools

> Has appropriate staff and staff organisation for documentation.

For major purchases, the user may also wish to carry out an audit of the supplier's quality system to ensure that the supplier's written standards and procedures are adhered to. Further audits may be advisable during the system development period to maintain confidence that the system is being produced in the approved manner.

8.3 Documentation management factors

Before placing a contract for an FVS (and, possibly, for an LVS), the user should investigate the way in which potential suppliers manage their documentation. The user should ask questions relating to the following key factors:

> The use of documentation standards

> The use of documentation procedures

> Documentation quality assurance and quality control

> The use of documentation methods, techniques and tools

> Staffing.

In some areas it may be sufficient for the user to check that the supplier uses good practices. In other areas (e.g. document presentation and electronic document preparation) the user may need to be satisfied that the supplier's standards and procedures are sufficiently flexible to meet the user's documentation requirements.

The main points to consider in relation to each factor are discussed in the following sections.

8.4 Documentation standards

The user should check that the supplier has standards relating to

Document types (see Section *8.4.1*)

Document to be supplied (see Section *8.4.2*)

Document structure (see Section *8.4.3*)

Diagramming notations (see Section *8.4.4*)

Document presentation (see Section *8.4.5*)

Document identification (see Section *8.4.6*)

Document copyright (see Section *8.4.7*)

Electronic document preparation (see Section *8.4.8*)

The use of international and national standards is recommended, but where no appropriate public standards exist suppliers should be working to their own standards.

8.4.1 Document types

The supplier may be expected to have a standard for the types of software document produced during project development, covering

The purpose or role of each document type

The scope and content of each document type

The inter-relationships between the document types

When and by whom the documents are produced.

Typical document types are those described in these Guidelines.

8.4.2 Documents to be supplied

The supplier may be expected to have a standard for the documentation supplied to users for different types of software product, covering

The documents supplied as standard

Any documents supplied as options

The provision for documentation maintenance

Pricing.

8.4.3 Document structure

Document structuring standards will cover such things as

How documents may be sub-divided (e.g. into chapters, sections, appendices)

The provision of reader access information (e.g. indexes)

Document front matter (preliminary pages, including title page and table of contents)

Document end matter (e.g. glossary, index, bibliography, reader comment form).

8.4.4 Diagramming notations

It is advisable for the supplier to have standards for the diagramming notations used in his documents, e.g.

Configuration diagrams

Design structure diagrams

System process diagrams

System data diagrams.

The notations used may relate to particular software engineering methods and associated tools (see Section *8.7*) and conform to appropriate, stated, standards.

8.4.5 Document presentation

Different production techniques and styles are often appropriate to different document types (e.g. typeset presentation for user reference and training documents and typewriter-style presentation for design, development and test documents). These differences should be reflected in the supplier's standards for document presentation.

Paper-based documents subject to frequent change should be produced in a loose-leaf format for ease of updating. Size of binders (e.g. A4 or A5) and the number of rings (e.g. 2, 3 or 4) are factors that may need to be considered to ensure compatibility between the supplier's and the user's documentation facilities.

The type of materials used for paper-based documentation may also need to be considered. For example, documents used outdoors may need to be printed on weather-proof materials.

Any requirement for the provision of documentation in electronic form (e.g. maintenance information on CD-ROM) may also impact on presentation standards.

8.4.6 Document identification

Document identification is a vital part of configuration management (see Section 9 of the Guidelines). The supplier must have a standard for the identification of his documents. This should include for each document

> Title
>
> Reference name/number
>
> Issue number
>
> Date of issue
>
> Issuing organisation identification
>
> Status (e.g. draft, approved)
>
> Security classification (e.g. confidential).

A standard method of uniquely identifying each page of a document is advisable, particularly where the document is to have loose-leaf binding.

8.4.7 Document copyright

The supplier should have a standard document copyright statement for each type of document, stating conditions for the use of the document (such as rights to copy) and any disclaimers of liability. If the user has ownership or use requirements other than those declared in the copyright statement, an alternative copyright should be negotiated as part of the contract conditions. See Section *3.3.7*.

8.4.8 Electronic document standards

With full variability systems, where suppliers and users may both contribute to the preparation and approval of documents, consideration should be given to the electronic exchange of documents between the supplier and the user. The user should check that the supplier's electronic documents can be processed on his own equipment. The contractual implications of any incompatibility should be carefully considered.

Where documentation is created or stored electronically, it is advisable to use international standards for open systems document interchange (e.g. the Standard Generalised Markup Language, ISO 8879). Documents may then be exchanged electronically between supplier and user without dependence on the use of particular documentation processing equipment or software.

8.5 Documentation procedures

Procedures are required for all stages of the documentation lifecycle (see Figure 3). The supplier should have procedures covering the following documentation processes:

Planning (see Section *8.5.1*)

Progress reporting (see Section *8.5.2*)

Preparation (see Section *8.5.3*)

Production (see Section *8.5.4*)

Review, validation and approval (see Section *8.5.5*)

Distribution (see Section *8.5.6*)

Recording (see Section *8.5.7*)

Storage (see Section *8.5.8*)

Updating (see Section *8.5.9*)

Archiving and disposal (see Section *8.5.10*)

The supplier should also have a means of ensuring that documentation procedures are adhered to. This may be done by supervision and review procedures within the project and by independent internal audit.

8.5.1 Documentation planning procedures

(1) **Documentation Requirements Specification**

For FPSs and LVSs the supplier will write his own specification of documentation requirements.

For FVSs, the user will normally specify his documentation requirements in the User Requirements Specification (see Section 3), and the supplier will respond to these requirements.

(2) **Documentation Design Specification**

The design of any software document (content, structure and appearance) should be specified and approved before the document is written.

(3) **Documentation Plan**

At the beginning of any software engineering project the supplier should produce a plan for software documentation, covering documentation extent (customer and internal documents), schedules, responsibilities and allocation of resources.

The plan should state

What documents are to be produced

How they are to be produced

When they are to be produced

Staff responsibilities for production (e.g. writing, reviewing, approving).

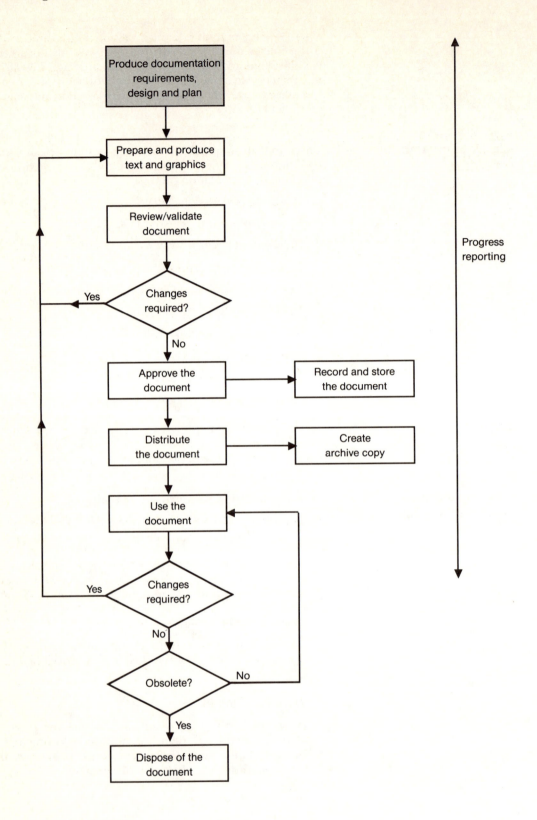

Figure 3   The Documentation Lifecycle

The documentation plan should be used to ensure that documents are produced, approved and used at the correct times in the development process.

The documentation plan may be incorporated in the project plan.

8.5.2 Progress reporting procedures

For effective monitoring and control of the documentation processes progress reporting procedures are required. These procedures may form part of the overall project management procedures.

Documentation progress reporting should be related to milestones in the documentation plan.

8.5.3 Preparation procedures

The supplier should have procedures for the creation and editing of the textual and graphical content of documents.

Preparation should proceed on the basis of an approved design specification and an approved documentation plan.

8.5.4 Production procedures

Procedures are required for the production of printed copies of any document (whether draft or approved). Methods of producing printed copies of textual and graphical material are required.

8.5.5 Review, validation and approval procedures

Review, validation and approval processes are essential in controlling the quality of documentation. They provide a means of checking

Accuracy, completeness and quality of content

Adherence to documentation standards.

Documents should be reviewed and approved for both technical accuracy and for the quality of presentation. Procedures should indicate how documents are to be reviewed (e.g. by inspection, analysis or testing).

Review, validation and approval should always be carried out by a person or persons other than the author of the document. The user may be included on the review authorisation panel for development documents which constitute project milestones (see Section 9).

Operational reference and training documents should be validated by testing them against the system they describe. Document testing should, therefore, form part of the overall system test procedures. Operational reference documents should be tested for correctness, completeness and ease of use.

The supplier should maintain a master copy of every approved document during the life of the project, to be updated by authorised personnel as required. If the user plans to maintain the documentation himself after system acceptance, he will also need to create a file of master copies.

8.5.6 Distribution procedures

Distribution of both draft and approved copies of documents should be controlled.

A project should maintain agreed distribution lists for its documents. A record should be kept of all dispatches (which version of which document on which date and to whom).

The supplier should have a means of ensuring that development work proceeds on the basis of accurate documentation (e.g. by ensuring that staff receive and work with the latest approved issue of any document).

8.5.7 Recording procedures

For every project, a record or index of all software documents should be maintained. The record should identify each document, its author and approver, its date of approval and issue, its distribution and its current status. See Section 9.

8.5.8 Storage procedures

Procedures are required for storing working and backup copies of current documents and for archiving non-active documents.

Security and safety factors should be taken into account, and the means provided of recreating documents should the master copies be lost or damaged (for example, by storing copies in separate locations).

While a project is active (i.e. until the end of system warranty), the supplier should keep a copy of superseded approved documents. This is to provide backwards traceability should errors occur, and to allow the reconstruction of earlier development states in the event of serious problems. With key contractual documents, such as functional specifications, it is advisable to keep a copy of all issues, whether draft or approved.

8.5.9 Updating procedures

Procedures are required for ensuring that changes made at any stage of the development process are accurately reflected in the documentation. See Section 9.

Authorisation of any change to software design or code should include an instruction to update the associated documentation.

All authorised copies (as shown on the document distribution list) should be updated to reflect the changes made to the master copy.

With development documents it is helpful if the supplier marks changes where they occur (e.g. by rules in the margin). As a minimum, an issue record or amendment notice should state in what ways the current issue of the document differs from the previous issue.

8.5.10 Archiving and disposal procedures

The supplier should have procedures for the storage and maintenance of documentation for an agreed period of time after the handover of a software product to the user.

Both the supplier and the user should have procedures for the disposal of obsolete documentation.

8.6 Documentation quality

Documentation should be subject to the supplier's quality assurance procedures. See Section 8.5.5 and Section 10.

8.7 Documentation methods, techniques and tools

Methods for documentation normally form part of particular software engineering methods (e.g. Yourdon, SSADM, Mascot). If a supplier uses an established method for developing software, then document types, content and use will largely be governed by that method.

Documentation techniques include

> Markup of document structure and/or formatting (e.g. the Standard Generalised Markup Language)

> Diagramming techniques (e.g. entity relationship diagrams, data flow diagrams)

> Formal languages (e.g. Pseudocode for design specification).

The use of automated tools that support documentation methods and techniques is strongly recommended, particularly where those tools support consistency-checking of the information content of the documents.

Where a supplier uses structured methods and supporting tools, the user can have greater confidence that accurate documentation will be produced and maintained, and that documentation standards will be consistently applied. He should also find that the speed of document production is faster than where unstructured and/or manual methods are used.

The user may need to ensure that electronic documents produced using automated tools can be processed on his own equipment (see *8.4.8*).

8.8 Staff Organisation and Responsibilities

The user should satisfy himself that the supplier's organisational structures are appropriate to the effectiveness of documentation processes (for example, in the provision of staff supervision).

The existence of a separate publications group or department is not essential to the production of good software documentation. However, the use of some specialist documentation staff within the organisation is advisable, to support the documentation efforts of system and software specialists.

Specialist documentation staff include

> Documentation managers

> Documentation consultants

> Documentation designers

> Authors

> Editors

> Illustrators.

The allocation of staff responsibilities for documentation, whether documentation specialists or not, should be clearly defined (in job descriptions, procedures or in project or documentation plans).

Staff should be trained in documentation methods and techniques and should be familiar with the organisation's documentation standards and procedures.

Section Nine: Configuration Management

9.1 Purpose of configuration management

Configuration management is the discipline which ensures that any proposed change to a system baseline definition or build level is prepared, accepted and controlled in accordance with set procedures. Changes to be controlled include corrections, modifications and enhancements. Configuration management applies equally to hardware, software and documentation.

For the use of a computer-based system, configuration management provides the means to:

(a) Ensure that all aspects of the delivered software and hardware are known and documented.

(b) Ensure that the hardware and software build of the delivered system is identical to (or can be related to) the state of the system when it was tested prior to delivery.

(c) Ensure that all documentation supplied is applicable to the delivered system and is maintained in line with any subsequent changes.

(d) Ensure that all delivered test and diagnostic programs relate correctly to the delivered build level, and are maintained in line with any subsequent changes.

(e) Enable design changes, corrections and enhancements to be carried out, tested and documented in a controlled, safe and orderly manner.

(f) Enable problems in operational service to be related to a defined set of documentation.

(g) Enable systems to be rebuilt and regenerated to an identical standard in the event of accidental loss or corruption.

The user can be certain of obtaining these benefits only if the supplier has already applied rigorous configuration control during the specification, design and development phases. The user should, therefore, specify this as a requirement in the User Requirements Specification, and should require evidence of its correct application by the supplier.

It is essential for the supplier to continue to apply configuration control procedures after delivery, in collaboration with the user. Similar control should also be exercised by the user for all interfacing plant equipment and for his own documentation prepared for operational or maintenance use.

9.1.1 Scope of the Guidelines The Guidelines discuss the principles of configuration management as they apply to software and to documentation.

9.2 Application to different types of system

The user should not assume that configuration management is required only for complex systems containing special-to-project software. All software, including environment and standard application software, is subject to change during the life of a project. Lack of control over the hardware, software and documentation of any system will inevitably lead to chaos, sooner or later.

Even so-called standard packages are rarely completely standard, and may be modified to meet some other user's requirement. Also faults may be discovered in software packages after many years of successful use, and elimination of these faults can lead to new problems arising. Users should consider entering into agreements with the supplier to ensure notification of the changes needed to correct such faults.

Changes or improvements in plant instrumentation or operating procedures can also lead to software changes being made.

9.3 Configuration management principles and procedures

9.3.1 Entities requiring control

The entities requiring control are:

Software modules

Software subsystems

Software libraries

Documentation

Physical media

External interfaces.

Entities identified for configuration control are called configuration items.

Modules

The software should be partitioned during the design process into modules, some of which represent the realisation of a requirement in the Functional Specification, and others of which support the overall system software facilities. In configuration management, the module is the smallest unit (or lowest level) which is referenced as a configuration item.

Subsystems

A group of software modules will interact together to form a subsystem which performs major functions. Functional or interface changes in a single module may thus cause changes to propagate throughout a subsystem.

Libraries

Software, even after completion of development, can exist in a number of versions to meet the requirements of different users or issues made during different phases of a project. During the development phase, it is necessary to preserve copies of program modules at various baseline stages, in order to be able to recreate later issues that may be lost or accidentally destroyed. Consequently, many different versions and issues of any module or program must be stored by the supplier in a library or archive, from which they can be retrieved on demand and integrated into a software system of known integrity. Archive copies of the associated documentation should also be kept.

Documentation

Keeping all documentation in step with changes is one of the most difficult aspects of configuration management, because of the relative ease with which software can be changed. Particular care should be taken to destroy working copies of obsolete issues of documents when changes are made (although an archive copy should be kept). Changes from one issue to the next should be marked in the documentation and a record should be kept of all changes implemented.

Physical media

Software in its physical realisation may be stored on magnetic disc (rigid or floppy), magnetic tape (reel or cassette), optical disc or PROM to facilitate revision. Paper tape and punched card media are obsolete.

Up-to-date copies of all software media must be kept and maintained. Copies of new issues and versions should be included in the library as they are released.

External interfaces

Software is designed to operate correctly in defined hardware environments, consisting of the computer itself and all connected peripherals, plant equipment interfaces and other connected systems and communications channels. Any changes to that environment can affect the correct functioning of the software. Consequently, configuration management must be applied to specifications of all connected systems and hardware items in order to cover any effects on the software resulting from external changes.

9.3.2 Identification methods

Software identification

All software media must be externally labelled to give a clear indication of their content. A standard form of labelling is preferable such as name, issue number, version number, date, inspection level. Machine-readable configuration items must contain the identification information in machine-readable form. This ensures that all copies of the item have the same identification.

Naming

A unique name must be assigned to every computer file or document produced. These may be specified in the Project Plan.

A naming convention that includes computer file names for all of the application software and documents, where relevant, is recommended. The names should indicate

> Module name or document type
>
> Type of file, e.g. source code, object code, data, text
>
> Any other identifying information which may be required, e.g. operating system naming conventions.

Inspection level

The inspection level information incorporated in the labelling is a means of identifying the status of a configuration item as it passes through a cycle of inspection stages. Typical inspection stages are:

Not inspected

Reviewed

Module tested

Integrated and system tested

Accepted for production use.

After any redesign, error correction or modification has been applied to an item, its inspection level and labelling must revert to the start of the cycle for review, revalidation and retest.

Document identification

All documents must have a unique title, reference name/number, issue number, date and status (e.g. draft, approved, confidential). In formatted documents it is advisable to repeat the reference and issue identification on each page, together with the page number, to ensure that each page is uniquely identifiable. The issue number must be changed each time changes are made to the document.

Variants of documents produced for different versions of a software release must be identified in a manner that allows them to be related to the appropriate software version.

Registration and indexing

A master index should be maintained which lists and uniquely identifies all configuration items which together define the current system configuration, including documentation. An up-to-date security copy of the index should always be maintained in a secure location.

The index should contain sufficient information on any configuration item to distinguish it from earlier or later issues and/or versions.

A record should be kept of any errors found and the corresponding corrections required in any configuration item.

Registration thus covers the cross-referencing of all items under configuration control to indicate their inter-relationships, interactions and usage.

9.3.3 Issue, release and version control

Software issue, release and version control

(a) **Module level**

Different issues of any software module arise during development as corrections are made or facilities added. Major issues of software are normally called releases or builds.

Different users of a standard package may require small variations, giving rise to different versions of a release.

All documentation relating to an issue, release or version must be uniquely identified in a way which is related to the issue, release or version of the corresponding software.

(b) **System level**

Issue, release and version control, as described above for modules, must also be applied at the various integration levels of subsystems and complete systems. This may involve separate system level and module level issue release and version numbers for all software and the associated documentation.

Documentation issue and version control

Issue control should start with the User Requirements Specification and the Functional Specification. All documents created during the project should be subjected to issue control, involving unique identification methods and formal procedures for preparing, authorising and promulgating changes. Draft issues as well as approved issues should be uniquely identified. See Section 8.

Record Keeping

In addition to the master index which defines the current system configuration, the supplier must keep a record of all issues, releases and versions of all configuration items. The record must include information such as identification, status, inter-relationship, project responsibility and physical location for each issue/release version of each item.

9.3.4 Procedures

Configuration management procedures fall under the headings of **Staff responsibilities, Reviews and inspections, Copying and storage, Archiving and disposal** and **Security.**

Staff responsibilities

The responsibilities of each category of staff involved in configuration management should be defined. This applies particularly to the supplier's staff who are responsible for authorising changes, inspection levels and releases. User's staff may also be involved in certain authorisation situations; their responsibilities and levels of authority should be clearly defined and agreed between user and supplier (see Section 3.)

The user should also obtain agreement on any division of responsibilities between user staff and supplier staff for technical back-up and for ongoing maintenance of the software and documentation after installation and acceptance. This may be the subject of a separate maintenance contract.

Reviews and inspections

A vital function in the quality control of any software engineering project is the institution of procedures for carrying out independent reviews and inspections of the work of the software designers and programmers. These procedures are equally applicable to initial design work and to any later corrections, modifications or enhancements.

(a) **Review procedures**

Reviews should be carried out by senior staff at all milestones in the development phase, and also during any major updates or enhancements to operational systems.

All documents prepared or amended at a project milestone should be circulated for review and comment to nominated reviewing authorities (which may include the user). A review meeting should follow, at which the originators or modifiers of the document can respond to queries, criticisms or objections. Following approval at a review meeting, the document is frozen and issued, when it becomes a new baseline definition.

A change proposal cycle should operate, which may lead to the approval of subsequent changes to the baseline document. See Section 8.

Reviewing teams are advised to work through prepared checklists to ensure that all aspects of the design are covered in a systematic manner. The development of such checklists for each stage of activity is an important function of quality management. See Section 10.

(b) **Inspection procedures**

Inspection takes place at a lower level than the review. It has the aim of eliminating errors in the software design specification, module design, module coding, test plan and test specifications.

It has particular value in enabling errors to be eradicated at the earliest possible stage in the development cycle, with important cost savings. It may also be applied to any modifications, corrections or enhancements which have to be made to a delivered system.

Copying and storage

Procedures are required for storing and retrieving documents and code from the software library. Procedures are also required for producing copies of stored material, taking into account authorisation and copyright restrictions.

Archiving and disposal

The supplier should have procedures for the storage and maintenance of documentation and software for an agreed period of time after the handover of a software product to the user.

Both the supplier and the user should have procedures for the disposal of obsolete configuration items.

Security

Software can be lost, stolen or destroyed, it can be modified by unauthorised action and it can be corrupted by software errors or hardware malfunctions. It is therefore of vital importance that any particular issue, release or version of a software system can be recreated without error.

This requires that exact archive copies of issues, releases or versions be made, verified and safely stored. Both suppliers and users should have adequate facilities and safeguards for generating copies, validating them and storing them in a safe location which is inaccessible to unauthorised persons. This last requirement may also be necessary for certain types of data.

9.3.5 Tools and automatic methods

Tools for automated configuration management are becoming more widely available and of increasing versatility. Facilities which can be provided include the following:

Automation of the library function covering software and documentation filestores

Control of access to library filestores

A basis for a secure issue/release/version control system

A basis for a secure change control system

Record maintenance for all configuration items

Documentation automatically kept in step with software changes

Facilities for software releases to be built and rebuilt under automatic control

Selected reports on demand

Simplification of accounting procedures.

Section Ten: Quality Assurance

10.1 Purpose of quality assurance

Quality assurance is the planned and systematic pattern of all actions necessary to establish adequate confidence that the product or service conforms to established technical requirements. This means ensuring that adequate quality control methods are in place and effective during the software lifecycle, to ensure that the user's requirements are fully satisfied.

Great emphasis is now being placed on quality assurance of software. This applies especially to safety-related real time systems where software is crucial to the safety of personnel and plant, in applications including, for example, the surveillance and control of major plant, vehicles (including aircraft and space vehicles), and also for all command and control systems. However, because software integrity and thus quality is considered equally important in many other areas of computing applications, quality assurance practices are being applied throughout the life cycle of all significant system or product developments.

10.1.1 Scope of the Guidelines

This Section deals with the documentation needed to achieve quality assurance in the planning and control of software. No particular set of procedures is assumed or recommended, and the documentation practices described here will have to be adjusted to the procedures of particular organizations and projects. However this will not require major effort, as the practices proposed are generic and relate to the common core of procedures, and indicate what might reasonably be expected in all cases.

10.2 Quality assurance programme

The dual aim of planning and quality control is the essence of quality assurance. The quality approach for software development will be centred around a Functional Specification which details how the user's requirements will be met. This will lead to documentation specifying exactly what is to be produced and giving precise details of the hardware and operational environment in which the software will run. The clear relationship between these different types of document forms the basis for the quality assurance programme.

Using the Functional Specification as a basis, evaluation is continually carried out and the results are compared to the objectives as defined in the Specification. Any deviation identified can then be rectified to ensure that the software system supplied meets the specification, or that any non-conformance to meet unforseen circumstance is brought to light for agreement.

10.3 Quality control organisation

The supplier should state clearly in the Quality Plan who will be responsible for the full implementation of all agreed system development and quality control procedures. These procedures will concern the means of developing, delivering, commissioning and testing the software to the agreed specifications.

10.4 Quality Plan

The Quality Plan should state the requirement for document review procedures. This will include resources, activities, tasks, milestones and monitoring considerations.

The quality control methods to be applied must be defined in the Quality Plan. This plan identifies standards, procedures, methods and tools to be used throughout the development to achieve the user's requirements.

The Quality Plan includes a list of the documentation required and references to the standards used at every stage of a project.

The contents of the Plan should be agreed at the start of a project between the supplier, the user, and, where appropriate, those responsible for post-installation maintenance. The Quality Plan must enable those charged with the control of the project to monitor the quality of the completed tasks and the relevance to the system of the duties performed in those tasks, and to ensure in all cases that these conform to the agreed specification.

The Quality Plan should therefore consist of:

A summarised list of the main tasks and product deliverables

A statement of the quality assurance organisation responsibilities and authorities

Details of, or reference to, the development methods, tools and procedures to be used to ensure that the quality aims will be met

A statement of the review policy to be adopted during all stages of the development process

A list of the documentation required for both development purposes and for delivery to the user

A statement of the controls exercised during the development process.

A Quality Plan gives the following benefits:

It provides the basis for implementation planning from the outset of the project

It encourages those involved to consider the full range of controls needed during the development process

It provides a framework within which all the parties concerned with the development can co-operate towards a successful and definable end to the project.

Section Eleven: Bibliography

BEAMA
  Contracts for the acquisition and utilisation of computer software for industrial control and monitoring systems. London: BEAMA, 1982 (BEAMA Legal Department Publication, 240).

British Standards Institution BS 0:Pt 1:1974
  Standard for standards: introduction to standardization. London: BSI, 1974.

British Standards Institution BS 1629:1989
  Recommendations for references to published materials. London: BSI, 1989.

British Standards Institution BS 1749:1985
  Alphabetical arrangement and the filing order of numbers and symbols. London: BSI, 1985.

British Standards Institution BS 3700:1988
  Preparation of indexes to books, periodicals and other publications. London: BSI, 1988.

British Standards Institution BS 5515:1984
  Code of practice for documentation of computer-based systems. London: BSI, 1984.

British Standards Institution BS 6529:1984
  Recommendations for examining documents, determining their subjects and selecting indexing terms. London: BSI, 1984.

Brockman, R. John
  Writing better computer user documentation. Chichester: Wiley, 1986.

EEUA
  Guide to user needs for technical documentation (engineering). London: EEUA, 1982 (EEUA Handbook no 36).

EEUA
  Guide to the engineering of microprocessor-based systems for instrumentation and control. London: EEUA, 1981 (EEUA Handbook no 38).

Electronic Engineering Association
  Assessment criteria for reviewing emerging standards, guidelines and codes of practice in safety critical systems. London: EEA, 1989.

Goodall, Hilary and Reilly, Susan S.
  Writing for the computer screen. London: Greenwoods, 1989.

Health and Safety Executive
  Programmable electronic systems in safety-related applications. 1—an introductory guide. London: HMSO, 1987.

Health and Safety Executive
Programmable electronic systems in safety-related applications.
2—general technical guidelines. London: HMSO, 1987.

IEEE
%   Software engineering standards. 3rd ed. New York: IEEE, 1989.

IEEE IEEE Std 729-1983
IEEE Standard glossary of software terminology (being revised as
IEEE Std P610.12). New York: IEEE, 1983.

IEEE IEEE Std 730-1984
IEEE Standard for software quality assurance plans (under revision).
New York: IEEE, 1984.

IEEE IEEE Std 828-1988
IEEE Standard for software management configuration plans [under
revision]. New York: IEEE, 1988.

IEEE IEEE Std 829-1983
IEEE Standard for software test documentation [under revision]. New
York: IEEE, 1983.

IEEE IEEE Std 830-1984*
IEEE Guide to software requirements specifications [under revision].
New York: IEEE, 1984.

IEEE IEEE Std 982.1-1988
IEEE Standard dictionary of measures to produce reliable software.
New York: IEEE, 1989.

IEEE IEEE Std 982.2-1988
Guide for the use of IEEE Standard dictionary of measures to produce
reliable software. New York: IEEE, 1989.

IEEE IEEE Std 983-1986*
IEEE Guide for software quality assurance planning. New York:
IEEE, 1986.

IEEE IEEE Std 1002-1987*
IEEE standard taxonomy for software engineering standards. New
York: IEEE, 1987.

IEEE IEEE Std 1008-1987*
IEEE Standard for software unit testing. New York: IEEE, 1987.

IEEE IEEE Std 1012-1986*
IEEE Standard for software verification and validation plans. New
York: IEEE, 1986.

IEEE IEEE Std 1016-1987*
IEEE Recommended practice for software design descriptions. New
York: IEEE, 1987.

IEEE IEEE Std 1028-1988*
IEEE Standard for software reviews and audits. Corrected edition.
New York: IEEE, 1989.

*%   *Items marked * are included in the compendium marked %*

IEEE IEEE Std 1042-1987*
    IEEE Guide to software configuration management. New York:
    IEEE, 1988.

IEEE IEEE Std 1058.1-1987*
    IEEE Standard for software project management plans. New York:
    IEEE, 1987.

IEEE IEEE Std 1063-1987*
    IEEE Standard for software user documentation. New York: IEEE,
    1987.

IEEE IEEE Std P 610.5
    IEEE Standard glossary of data management (in preparation). New
    York: IEEE,

IEEE IEEE Std P 610.7
    IEEE Standard glossary of computer networking (in preparation).
    New York: IEEE,

IEEE IEEE Std P 610.9
    IEEE Standard glossary of computer security and privacy (in
    preparation). New York: IEEE,

IEEE IEEE Std P 610.10
    IEEE Standard glossary of computer hardware (in preparation). New
    York: IEEE,

IEEE IEEE Std P 610.12
    IEEE Standard glossary of software engineering (in preparation).
    New York: IEEE,

IEEE IEEE Std P 610.13
    IEEE Standard glossary of programming languages (in preparation).
    New York: IEEE,

IEEE IEEE Std P 828
    Standard for software configuration management plans (in
    preparation). New York: IEEE,

IEEE IEEE Std P 1016.2
    Guide to software design descriptions (in preparation). New York:
    IEEE, 1989.

IEEE IEEE Std P 1059
    Guide to software verification and validation plans (in preparation).
    New York: IEEE,

ISO ISO 646:1983
    Information processing—ISO 7-bit coded character set for
    information interchange. 2nd ed. Geneva: ISO, 1983.

ISO ISO 2382
    Data processing—vocabulary. Geneva: ISO, various dates.

ISO ISO 3511/1-1977 BS 1646:Pt 4:1984
    Symbolic representation for process measurement, control functions
    and instrumentation: Part 4. London: BSI, 1984.

*Items marked * are included in the compendium marked % on previous page*

ISO ISO 5807-1985 BS 4058:1987
Data processing flowchart symbols, rules and conventions. London: BSI, 1987.

ISO ISO 6592-1985
Information processing—Guidelines for the documentation of computer-based application systems. Geneva: ISO, 1985.

ISO ISO 7498:1984
Information processing systems—Open Systems Interconnection—Basic Reference Model. Geneva: ISO, 1984 (addendum 1987).

ISO ISO 8859-6:1987
Information processing systems—computer system configuration diagram symbols and conventions. Geneva: ISO, 1987.

ISO ISO 8879-1987 BS 6868:1987
Standard generalized markup language (SGML) for text and office systems. London: BSI, 1986.

Institution of Electrical Engineers
Guidelines for assuring testability. London: IEE, 1988.

Institution of Electrical Engineers
Software quality assurance: model procedures. London: IEE, 1990 (in press).

Martin, James
Recommended diagramming standards for analysts and programmers. London: Prentice-Hall, 1986.

Ministry of Defence DefStan 0016
Guide to the achievement of quality in software. Glasgow: Ministry of Defence, Feb 1984.

Ministry of Defence DefStan 0031
Development of safety critical software for airborne systems (interim standard-under revision). Glasgow: MoD, July 1987.

Ministry of Defence DefStan 0055
Requirements for the procurement of safety critical software in defence equipment (draft proposal). Glasgow: MoD, May 1989.

Ministry of Defence DefStan 0056
Requirements for the analysis of safety critical hazards equipment (draft proposal). Glasgow: MoD, May 1989.

Ministry of Defence JSP 188
Requirements for the documentation of software in military operational real time computer systems. 4th ed. London: MoD, 1987.

STARTS
IT-STARTS developers' guide. Manchester: National Computing Centre, STARTS Secretariat, Mar 1989.

STARTS
STARTS guide. 2nd ed. Manchester: National Computing Centre, STARTS Secretariat, 1987.

STARTS
STARTS purchasers' handbook: procuring software-based systems. 2nd ed. Manchester: National Computing Centre, STARTS Secretariat, 1989.

Stallings, William et al
Handbook of computer communications standards. London: Collier Macmillan, 1988, 3 v.

Strom, Jim
LAN standards: matter of protocols. Systems International, Dec 1988. 41,43,44,47,49.

Weiss, Edmond H.
How to write a usable user manual, Philadelphia: ISI Press, 1985.

Section Twelve: Glossary

3GL See *high-level language*.

4GL See *fourth generation language*.

acceptance The act by which the user indicates to the supplier that the agreed goods and services have been provided satisfactorily. It is quite common for acceptance to be agreed with minor defects and omissions identified, but with an understanding that these will be corrected by an agreed date.

acceptance testing Formal testing conducted to determine whether or not a system satisfies its acceptance criteria and hence to enable the user to determine whether or not to accept the system.

access security Hardware or software features, operating procedures or management procedures designed to permit authorised access and prevent unauthorised access to a computer system.

accuracy The ratio of error to total value. It is usually expressed as a percentage.

adaptability The ease with which software allows differing system constraints and user needs to be satisfied.

address The location of data or instructions in a computer's store. Note that data can be referred to by a virtual address during use. Such virtual addresses are real addresses but refer to memory space allocated under the control of an operating system to different users at different times.

algorithm A series of instructions or procedural steps for the solution of a specific problem, such as the evaluation of sines.

alpha-numeric Consisting of alphabetical and numerical symbols used in character sets, codes or files of data.

analogue to digital converter Also called *A to D converter, A/D converter* or *ADC*. A device which converts a voltage or current into a binary number for processing by a digital system. The converter may be hardware or a combination of hardware and software.

annunciator An audible or visible alarm device for attracting the attention of an operator.

application language A problem-oriented language whose statements contain or resemble the terminology of the occupation or profession of the user.

application software Software specifically produced for the functional use of a computer system (contrast with *environment software*).

AQAP Allied Quality Assurance Procedure. A series of NATO standards.

archiving The transfer of current operational data and software to a permanent storage medium to allow later regeneration in case of corruption or loss (or may be required for audit purposes).

as-built system The tested and approved system with all supporting documentation, supplies and spares.

ASCII American Standard Code for Information Interchange, representing letters, numbers, etc. by the 128 permutations of a 7-bit code.

assembler A program which converts instructions written in mnemonics.

assembly language A computer-oriented language where instructions are usually in one-to-one correspondence with computer instructions.

asynchronous A timing system in which each event or the performance of each operation starts as a result of a signal generated by the completion of the previous event or operation, or on the availability of those parts of the system required for the next event or operation.

audit An independent review for the purpose of assessing compliance with software requirements, specifications, baselines, standards, procedures, instructions, codes and contractual and licensing requirements.

automatic Pertaining to a process or device that, under specified conditions, functions without human intervention.

automatic control (mode) Control of a process by automatic means.

automation The process of controlling machinery or equipment by computer.

auxiliary store See *backing store*.

availability The ratio of system up-time to total operating time.

backing store Hardware used to retain data over long periods of time, and accessed by the central processor through input/output channels. Contrast with *memory*.

back-up Provisions made for the recovery of data files or software, for restart of processing, or for use of alternative equipment or procedures after a system failure.

baud A unit of signalling speed equal to the number of discrete signal events per second. Note that baud is only equivalent to bits per second for two-state signalling. Higher bit rates can be obtained by multi-level signalling.

baseline A specification or build of a computer system that has been formally reviewed and agreed upon, and which thereafter serves as a basis for further development, and which can be changed only through formal change control procedures.

benchmark A standard or point of reference against which a particular feature of a system is measured. The usual benchmark tests are those which compare different computers with each other using the criteria of speed of operation, throughput, responses, etc.

binary coded decimal (BCD) A notation in which each decimal digit is represented by a four-bit binary numerical, e.g. the number twenty three is represented by 0010 0011 (compare its representation 10111 in the pure binary numeration system).

bit	A contraction of the term binary digit: a unit of information represented by either a zero or a one.
BS	British Standard.
BSI	British Standards Institution.
build	An operational version of a software product/system incorporating a specified subset of the capabilities that the final product/system will include.
bus	A signal path carrying digital signals common to two or more nodes (see *data highway*).
CAMAC	Computer Aided Measurement and Control. CAMAC is a standard for equipment that connects computers to other external instrumentation equipment.
CASE	Computer-Aided Software Engineering.
CASE tool	Any computer-based tool that can assist in any aspect of software engineering. Tools are available for analysis and design, coding and testing, production of documentation, language development, database management, project management, configuration management, change control, etc. See *software tool* and *tool*.
CCITT	Consultative Committee International Telegraph and Telephone. A committee within the International Telecommunications Union. It concerns itself with the conventions which enable transfer of data between electronic systems. Its most well known series of recommendations are its 'V' series and X25 specifications. These conventions are commonly referred to in user requirements specifications and supplier tenders.
CD-ROM	Compact discs used as a data source for information search and retrieval by computer. Data is stored on such discs by a special process in a one-off operation. It is not possible to write data directly to CD-ROM from a computer or to store data on the disc in a cumulative fashion. See also *WORM*.
channel	A signal communication path or a functional unit that handles the transfer of data between sub-units of a system.
change control	The process by which a change is proposed, evaluated, approved or rejected, scheduled and tracked.
code	A set of unambiguous rules specifying the manner in which data may be represented in a discrete form, e.g. character code.
command language	A set of procedural operations with a related syntax, used to indicate the functions to be performed by an operating system.
common mode noise rejection	The ratio of the common interference voltage of the signal leads to earth at the input of a circuit to the common interference voltage measured at the output of the circuit with respect to the same earth.
common mode voltage	The common potential of the input signals with respect to earth (assuming a balanced differential input).
compile	To translate a higher order language program into machine code. Contrast with *interpret*.
compiler	A computer program used to compile.

computer system	A functional unit, consisting of one or more computers and associated software, that uses common storage for all or part of a program and also for all or part of the data necessary for the execution of the program, that executes user-written or user-designated programs, that performs user-designated data manipulation, including arithmetic operations and logic operations, and that can execute programs that modify themselves during their execution. A computer system may be a standalone unit or may consist of several interconnected units.
concurrency	The ability to execute processes in parallel on multiple processors or asynchronously on a single processor. Concurrent processes may interact with each other, and one process may suspend execution pending receipt of information from another process on the occurrence of an external event.
configuration	The totality of the hardware, software, firmware, services and supplies required for the successful operation of a computer-based system or associated group of systems at a given reference point in time.
configuration control	The process of evaluating, approving or disapproving and co-ordinating changes to configuration items after formal establishment of their configuration identification.
configuration identification	The process of designating the configuration items in a system and recording their characteristics.
configuration item	A collection of hardware, software or documentation elements treated as a unit for the purposes of configuration management.
configuration management	The process of identifying and defining the configuration items in a system, controlling the release and change of these items throughout the system lifecycle, recording and reporting the status of configuration items and change requests, and verifying the completeness and correctness of configuration items.
data	A representation of facts, concepts or instructions in a formalised manner suitable for communication, interpretation or processing by human or automatic means.
data acquisition	A general term for the capture of data from various sensors and the processing of the data for presentation to the operator in the form of VDU displays, printed logs, charts, etc.
database	A collection of data organised in interconnecting and interacting files.
data dictionary	A collection of the names of all data items used in a software system, together with the relevant properties of those items; for example, length of data item, representation, etc.
data flow	The flow of data through a system of processes, showing how the processes are connected.
data flow diagram	A graphic representation of a system showing data sources, data destinations, storage and processes performed on data as nodes and showing logical flow of data as links between the nodes.
data framing	The process of selecting the bit grouping representing one or more characters from a continuous stream of bits.

data highway	A link connecting a number of electronic devices (e.g. computers) by means of which the devices pass information to each other. Since all devices use the same physical link there must be a convention followed by each device which manages data collisions on the highway and which ensures that each recipient of data recognises the data meant for it.
data structure	A formalised representation of the ordering and accessibility relationships between data items without regard to their actual storage configuration.
decision table	A presentation in either matrix or tabular form of a set of conditions and their corresponding actions.
default value	A parameter value available to software for use where a particular signal input value is found to be outside its allowed range, or when the signal is not available.
deliverable	An intermediate or end product produced during the system lifecycle which forms part of the contractual supply of a system, for example, a Functional Specification, a System Test Specification, a software system, user documentation.
design	The process of defining the architecture, components, modules, interfaces, test approach and data for a computer system to satisfy specified requirements.
design analysis	The evaluation of a design or alternative designs to determine correctness with respect to stated requirements, conformance to design standards, system efficiency and other criteria.
design language	A language with special constructs and, sometimes, verification protocols, used to develop, analyse and document a design.
design method	A systematic approach to creating a design, consisting of the ordered application of a specific collection of tools, techniques and guidelines. See *development method.*
design requirement	Any requirement that impacts or constrains the design of a system or system component; for example, functional requirements, physical requirements, performance requirements, development standards, quality assurance standards.
design review	The formal review of an existing or proposed design for the purpose of detection and remedy of design deficiencies that could affect fitness for use and environmental aspects of the product or process, and/or for identification of potential improvements of performance, safety and economic aspects.
design specification	A specification that documents the design of a system or system component; for example, a software configuration item. Typical contents include system or component algorithms, control logic, data structures, data set use information, input/output formats and interface descriptions.
detailed design	The process of refining and expanding the preliminary design to contain more detailed descriptions of the processing logic, data structures and data definitions, to the extent that the design is sufficiently complete to be implemented.
development method	A systematic approach to the creation of software that defines development stages and specifies the activities, products, verification procedures and completion criteria for each stage.

development process   The process by which user needs are translated into software requirements, requirements are translated into design, the design is implemented in code, and the code is tested, documented and certified for operational use.

diagnostic program   A computer program that recognises, locates and explains either a fault in equipment or a mistake in a program.

digital to analogue converter   Also called *D to A converter, D/A converter* or *DAC*. A hardware device which converts a binary signal to an equivalent analogue (voltage or current) value.

disk storage   Storage on a magnetic disk (see *magnetic disk*).

display hierarchy   A linked sequence of system displays. For example, a plant overview display from which may be selected enlarged and more detailed sectional displays of individual subsystems.

document   A data medium and the data recorded on it, that generally has permanence and that can be read by humans or machines.

documentation   Any textual or pictorial information describing, defining, specifying, reporting or certifying activities, requirements, procedures or results.

documentation management   The management of documents, which may include the actions of identifying, acquiring, processing, storing and disseminating them.

documentation plan   A documentation plan defines the complete range of documents to be produced, including the method and timing of production for each document and the associated staff responsibilities.

downtime   The period during which a system is non-functional.

dump   To write the contents of a store, or part of a store, to an external medium.

duplex   A communication channel or circuit capable of conducting signals in both directions simultaneously, e.g. send and receive signals in telephony. Contrast with *simplex* and *half-duplex*.

encryption   The coding of a clear text message or signal to prevent unauthorised eavesdropping.

environment software   The total software which provides an operating environment for application software. It includes the operating system and other usually standard software components such as language interpreters, database management packages and other run-time utility software.

EPROM   Erasable Programmable Read Only Memory. A read-only memory in which stored data can be erased by ultra-violet light or other means and reprogrammed bit by bit with appropriate voltage pulses.

ergonomic design   Design for efficiency and ease of use, e.g. most frequently used keys within easy reach of the operator, or VDU screens readily discernible in ambient light conditions and with formats arranged for ready recognition of critical information.

error correction   A technique for automatically detecting and correcting errors occurring in the generation or transmission of a digital signal by the addition of a number of redundant bits.

Ethernet   A local area network using baseband signalling on a co-axial cable.

expert system	A system which employs a store of knowledge provided by human experts in order to make value judgements and best guesses in arriving at a solution to a problem.
fall-back control	Provision made for the use of alternative hardware or procedures in the event of a system failure.
feasibility study	A study to identify and analyse the problems associated with an outline proposal for a system development project in order to demonstrate its viability, costs and benefits.
file	A set of related data records.
firmware	Computer programs and data loaded into a read-only memory.
fleeting signal	A transient signal of short duration.
floating point arithmetic	Arithmetic based on floating point numbers, i.e. numbers represented by two parts, a fixed point part, and a characteristic or exponent.
floppy disk	See *magnetic disk*.
flowchart	A diagrammatic representation of the definition, analysis or solution of a problem in which symbols are used to represent operations, data, flow and equipment.
formal language	A language whose rules are explicitly established prior to its use, e.g. programming language. Contrast with *natural language*.
fourth-generation language	A programming language which enables processes which would require several *high level language* statements to be represented in a single statement. These languages are commonly specific to a particular kind of range of applications.
FPS	Fixed Program System. A standard product with no facility for functional variation by individual users.
freeze date	The date beyond which no changes to a specification or formal report will be accepted.
function	A specific purpose of an entity or its characteristic action.
functional decomposition	A method of designing a system by breaking it down into its components in such a way that the components correspond directly to system functions and subfunctions.
functional design	The design of the functional units of a system restricted to its functional aspects as opposed to the physical ones.
functional requirement	A requirement that specifies a function that a system or system component must be capable of performing.
functional specification	A specification that defines the functions that a system or system component must perform.
FVS	Full Variability System. A system produced specifically for particular users, with potential for future modification by those users to meet changing requirements.
gateway	A linking facility which adapts the protocols and conventions of one network to that of another network, or to those of several networks.

graceful degradation	The ability of a system to continue to operate at a reduced efficiency or with limited functionality in the event of system failure.
Gray code	A binary code for consecutive numbers in which only one bit changes for each sequential change of number.
global data	Data required by a software module but not defined and used in that module alone.
half-duplex	A transmission path or circuit capable of transmitting data or information in either direction, but in only one direction at a time.
hard copy	Human-readable information storage, such as typewritten or machine printed characters on paper, or information stored on microfilm.
hard disk	See *magnetic disk*.
hardware	Computer equipment
hard-wired	Equipment wired to carry out a specific task or tasks.
help routine	An operator interface facility provided to assist users in the use of a system or system feature, or to explain features in more detail than is possible in the normal operator interface.
high level language	A programming language that does not reflect the structure of any one type of computer, and that can be used to write machine-independent source programs e.g. BASIC, FORTRAN.
historical data	A permanent record of data generated over a period of time during the operation of a system.
host	A computer used to prepare programs for use on another, usually smaller, computer system.
identifier	A symbol used to name, indicate or locate.
IEEE	Institute of Electrical and Electronics Engineers (USA).
initialisation	The action of setting a system to the state required for it to begin normal operation.
inspection	A formal evaluation technique in which software requirements, design or code are examined in detail by a person or group other than the author to detect faults, violations of development standards and other problems.
integrity	The ability of a system to maintain error-free operation.
integration	The stepwise linking and testing of system components to the whole system.
integration testing	An orderly progression of testing in which software elements, hardware elements or both are combined and tested until the entire system has been integrated. See also *system testing*.
interface	The point of interconnection between two systems or two parts of a system or between a person and a system. It is also used to mean the special logic, buffers, handshake arrangements, etc. that may be required to maintain effective communication between systems or parts of a system.

interpret	To translate and execute each source language statement of a program before translating and executing the next statement. Contrast with *compile*.
interpreter	A program used to interpret.
interrupt	A suspension of a process caused by an event external to that process and performed in such a way that the process can be resumed.
intrinsic safety	A high degree of safety built into designs to meet statutory and other codes and standards concerning design, operation and maintenance.
IPSE	Integrated Project Support Environment. A set of integrated CASE tools that supports the management of an information system engineering project, including tools for estimating, planning, control, configuration management, quality management, etc.
ISO	International Organization for Standardization.
isolation	The electrical separation of two or more circuits by the use of isolating devices such as transformers or optical couplers. Usually employed as a safety feature for the protection of circuit components or as a means of increasing the common mode voltage tolerance of a circuit.
issue level	The specification level of a software product at the time of release. See *software release*.
joystick	A control lever which can be rotated through 360°. This rotation is converted into electrical signals which define the lever's exact position to an intelligent device. This position is interpreted as an instruction from the operator.
kernel (software)	The nucleus or core of an operating system.
ladder diagram	A schematic representation of a logical circuit. The interconnection of the relay contacts and coils between the supply voltage rails are arranged to appear like the rungs of a ladder.
LAN	Local Area Network. A computer system with terminals located in different parts of a building, factory or small locality and linked by a communications network.
language	See *application language, formal language, fourth-generation language, high level language, low level language, natural language, programming language*.
latch	An electronic trigger circuit having two stable states, used to staticise a transient signal.
LED	Light-Emitting Diode, used as a coloured indicator on a control panel.
library	A formal and centralised collection of programs or data files written for a computer system.
life cycle	A succession of discrete activities or phases covering the total life of a project from initial conception to disposal.
light pen	A pen-shaped device which enables an operator to digitise a physical position on a cathode ray rube (CRT) display.
linkage editor/linker	A program used to create one load program from one or more independently produced object programs or load programs. This is done by resolving cross-references among the object programs, and possibly by relocating elements.

listing	Computer output in the form of a printed human-readable list.
log	A timed record of events and physical conditions within a system.
look-up table	A stored matrix of data for reference purposes.
low level language	A programming language that reflects the structure of a given type of computer, e.g. the machine code or assembler for a particular computer.
LVS	Limited Variability System. A standard product having some facility for variation to meet individual requirements.
magnetic disk	A revolving flat circular plate (hard or flexible "floppy") coated with a magnetizable surface layer on which data can be stored by magnetic recording.
magnetic tape	A reel or cassette of tape with a magnetizable surface layer on which data can be stored by magnetic recording.
maintenance	Any activity intended to retain a functional unit in, or to restore it to, a state in which it can perform its required function. Maintenance includes keeping a functional unit in a specified state by performing activities such as tests, measurements, replacements, adjustments and repairs.
maintenance plan	A document that identifies the management and technical approach that will be used to maintain software. Typically included are topics such as tools, resources, facilities and schedules.
manual operation/mode	Control of a process or system by manual methods, e.g. in the event of failure of automatic control.
main store	See *memory*.
maintainability	The ease with which maintenance of a functional unit can be performed in accordance with prescribed requirements. It may also be defined as the probability that a failed functional unit will be returned to operational effectiveness within a given period of time.
mass storage	The general term for high capacity computer memory which contains programs and date which must be transferred to the lower capacity main memory of the computer before it can be processed. The mass storage may take many forms, e.g. disk, magnetic tape and bubble memory.
memory	Internal storage, that which is accessible by a computer without the use of input-output channels, used to store data and instructions during processing. Also called main store, primary storage.
method	An organised collection of procedures, notations and techniques; for example, structured analysis. See *design method* and *development method*.
microcomputer	A system which contains a microprocessor and its associated memory, backing store, data buses and interface units which enables it to run programs and to communicate with external devices.
microprocessor	A central processing unit of a computer system, fabricated in a single chip. It comprises an arithmetic and logic unit (ALU), a control unit, registers and interfaces to external devices such as memory.
milestone	A scheduled event for which some project member or manager is held accountable and that is used to measure progress; for example, a formal review, issuance of a specification, product delivery.

model	A representation of a real world process, device or concept, e.g. conceptual model, analytical model, reliability model.
modem	An acronym for MOdulator/DEModulator. It causes a series of binary values to affect a high frequency carrier signal in a prescribed way (modulation) so that communication can take place with a remote device which retrieves the original binary value from the high frequency signal (demodulation).
module	See *program module*.
multiplex	To share one device or communication channel between several tasks or signals.
multi-tasking	Refers to the capability of a system to support two or more active tasks simultaneously.
natural language	A language whose rules are based on current usage without being explicitly prescribed, e.g. English, French. Contrast with *formal language*.
network	A system involving two or more processors and terminals interconnected so that they may share resources (hardware, software and data). See also *LAN*, *VAN* and *WAN*.
node	In a network, a point where one or more functional units interconnect with transmission lines.
noise characteristics	The features of any induced effect on an electrical signal, e.g. frequency, amplitude, relationship with normal or ideal signal.
noise, electrical	The unwanted component of a signal.
normal mode	See *series mode*.
object program/code	A program which a computer can use directly without the need of a compiler or assembler. It is usually the output of a compiler or assembler which uses a source program/code as input.
OCR	Optical Character Recognition. Recognition by machine of written or printed characters.
on-line	The operation of a computer to control a functional unit directly, e.g. continuous control of a furnace temperature.
operational data (file)	Data essential to the normal operation of a system.
operating system	Software for controlling the execution of computer programs which may provide scheduling, debugging, input/output control, accounting, compilation, storage allocation, data management and related services. See *environment software*.
OSI	Open Systems Interconnection. A developing set of international standards aimed at making it possible for all computer systems to intercommunicate.
out-of-alarm procedure	A procedure for resetting the system after clearing an alarm state.
overlaid store	The technique of repeatedly using the same areas of internal storage during different stages of a program.

over-ride
The temporary suspension of an automatic control function and its replacement by manual control.

parity
A single-bit extension to a field of binary data. It indicates whether there is an odd or even number of ones in the binary field. It thus enables error checking of the data field prior to processing of the data.

parameter
A variable that is given a constant value for a specific application.

performance
A measure of the ability of a computer system or subsystem to perform its functions; for example, response time, throughput, number of transactions.

peripheral
Any equipment, distinct from the control processing unit, which may provide the system with outside communication or additional facilities.

PERT
Project Evaluation and Review Technique; a project management method.

PES
Programmable Electronic System.

plant
A general term used to define the users' equipment and processes from which data is derived by the computer system and to which control signals are directed.

plotter
A peripheral which converts signals issued by the computer into graphical form on paper.

polling
A process that involves interrogating in succession every terminal on a shared communication line for transferring data or control signals.

port
A point at which signals can enter or leave a functional unit.

portability
The ease with which software can be transferred from one computer system or environment to another.

preliminary design
The process of analysing design alternatives and defining the software architecture. Preliminary design typically includes definition and structuring of computer program components and data, definition of the interfaces, and the preparation of timing and sizing estimates.

primary storage
See *memory*.

problem oriented language (POL)
A *high level language* designed specifically for the treatment of a particular task, e.g. COBOL for commercial work and FORTRAN for mathematical and scientific tasks. Many process control systems are provided with the supplier's own language tailored to the particular needs of control tasks.

procedure
A portion of a program which is named and which performs a specific task.

program
A sequence of coded instructions fed into a computer, enabling it to perform specified logical and arithmetical operations on data.

program library
An organised collection of computer programs.

programmable logic controller (PLC)
A computer system able to accept digital inputs and which can be programmed to perform logical operations (including time delays) on these inputs prior to outputting digital control signals to the plant. It is user-programmable using a simple problem oriented language and is often used to replace relay circuitry for the control of industrial processes.

programming language
A systematic and formally structured means of communicating instructions and data to a computer. Languages may be user-oriented and 'English like', i.e. *high level languages* such as BASIC or FORTRAN. They may also be more closely associated with the way the computer works, i.e. *low level languages* such as Assembler, or created for a particular range of applications (*fourth generation languages*).

programming support environment
An integrated collection of tools accessed via a single command language to provide programming support capabilities throughout the system lifecycle. The environment typically includes tools for designing, editing, compiling, loading, testing, configuration management and project management. Often referred to as IPSE.

program module
A logically separable part of a program.

PROM
Programmable Read Only Memory. A memory component into which information can be written after the device is manufactured, but thereafter cannot be altered.

project plan
A management document describing the approach that will be taken for a project. The plan typically describes the work to be done, the resources required, the methods to be used, the configuration management and quality assurance procedures to be followed, the schedules to be met, the project organisation, etc.

protocol
A set of conventions between communicating processes on the format and content of messages to be exchanged.

prototype
A system implementation produced rapidly from a preliminary specification and from which improved versions are developed and tried, leading to the development of a fully operational system.

pseudocode
A combination of programming language and natural language used for software design.

QA
See *quality assurance*.

quality
The totality of features and characteristics of a product or service that bears on its ability to satisfy given needs.

quality assurance
The planned systematic activities necessary to provide adequate confidence that a component or system conforms to established technical requirements.

quality control
The use of standards, formal reviews and configuration control undertaken to ensure that all components of a software system are correct and complete.

quality metric
A quantitative measure of the degree to which software possesses a given attribute that affects its quality.

quality plan
A quality plan defines the technical, documentation and review requirements needed to ensure control of quality.

RAM
Random Access Memory. A computer memory array in which data is stored in such a way that it can be accessesd randomly by the computer without processing previously written data (unlike serial access media such as magnetic tape).

real time
Pertaining to the processing of data by a computer in connection with another process outside the computer according to time constraints imposed by the outside process. This term is also used to describe systems operating in conversational mode, and processes that can be influenced by human intervention while they are in progress.

real time system
A computer system which interchanges information with another system within time limits determined by the other system.

record
A collection of related data or words treated as a unit.

redundancy
The inclusion of duplicate or alternate system elements to improve operational reliability by ensuring continued operation in the event that a primary element fails.

relation
In a relational database, a group of data which can be represented as a table in which the columns contain values of attributes and the rows represent tuples (or records).

relational database
A database in which data is held in a number of linked relations (qv) to avoid redundancy and to facilitate its maintenance.

release
See *software release*.

reliability
See *software reliability*.

requirement
A condition or capability that must be met or possessed by a system or system component to satisfy a contract, standard, specification, or other formally imposed document. The set of all requirements forms the basis for subsequent development of the system or system component.

requirements analysis
The process of studying user needs to arrive at a definition of a system or software requirements.

requirements specification
A specification that sets forth the requirements for a system or system component; for example, a software configuration item. Typically included are functional requirements, performance requirements, interface requirements, design requirements and development standards.

resolution
The accuracy to which a value is held in memory; the accuracy to which a continuously variable analogue parameter can be represented digitally.

resolution timing
The time interval between samples of analogue data.

response time
The elapsed time between the end of a stimulus to a computer system and the start of the response.

RF
Radio Frequency.

robotics
The application of control technology to manipulative activities such as holding, lifting, rotating, placing, conveying.

ROM
Read Only Memory. A memory component containing information built-in at the time of manufacture which cannot be subsequently altered.

routine
A program, or part of a program, that may have some general or frequent use.

secondary storage
See *backing store*.

security
The protection of computer hardware and software from accidental or malicious access, use, modification, destruction or disclosure.

self-optimising

The ability of a system to modify certain internal parameters in the light of changed external conditions in order to maintain the required level of functionality.

sensor

A detector which transduces physical parameters such as temperature, pressure and position to signals which can be read by a computer system.

series mode rejection

The ratio of the series mode noise voltage across the input of a circuit to the residual interference voltage at the output.

series mode voltage

The voltage measured across the input of a circuit.

sequence control

Control by which the controller outputs digital control signals in a calculated sequence and at calculated time intervals.

SGML

Standard Generalised Markup Language. A language for specifying the logical structure of documents independently of how those documents are formatted, thereby permitting the electronic interchange of documents between different document processing systems. The language falls within the Application Layer (Layer 7) of the Open Systems Interconnection (OSI) model.

shut-down

A procedure to shut off and close down a system in a safe manner without undue loss of material, equipment or data; can be used as a routine measure or in an emergency.

simplex

A transmission path or circuit which permits transmission in one direction only.

signal conditioning

The process of filtering and purifying a signal. It is used to eliminate power surges or unwanted disturbances (harmonics or induced voltages) so that the signal reflects the true value of the information it is intended to convey.

simulation

The representation of physical phenomena by means of operations performed by a computer system.

soak test

The process of submitting a system to continual working under a prespecified environment and workload for a predetermined duration. It may include operation at an abnormally high temperature.

software

Computer programs. The term is also applied to the associated program descriptions and listings and to copies of programs on all types of medium.

software development process See *development process*.

software engineering

The systematic approach to the analysis, design, development, installation, operation, maintenance and retirement of software.

software quality

The composite characteristics of software that determine the degree to which the software in use will meet the expectations of the customer.

software release

The issue of a program or set of programs for general use, following validation.

software reliability

The probability that software will not cause the failure of a system for a specified time under specified conditions. The probability is a function of the inputs to and use of the system as well as a function of the existence of faults in the software. The inputs to the system determine whether existing faults, if any, are encountered.

software tool	A computer program used to help develop, test, analyse or maintain another computer program or its documentation; for example, automated design tool, compiler, test tool, maintenance tool. See *CASE tool*.
source (code) listing	A listing of the content of a source program.
source program	A computer program that must be compiled, assembled or interpreted before being executed by a computer.
specification	A document that prescribes, in a complete, precise, verifiable manner, the requirements, design, behaviour or other characteristics of a system or a system component.
specification language	A language, often a machine-processable combination of natural and formal language, used to specify the requirements, design, behaviour, or other characteristics of a system or system components.
stand-alone (system)	A system which operates in isolation, e.g. an intelligent VDU may operate either as a stand alone computer system or as a peripheral to a large computer system.
stand-by (mode)	Equipment or procedures available for bringing into immediate use in the event of a failure in the primary system.
start-up	A procedure to initialise and power-up a system in a systematic and safe manner from the cold state.
state-driven	The consequential execution of specific software operations dependent on the binary state of input parameters.
store, storage	hardware used to retain data in machine-readable store. See also *backing store, memory*.
structured software	A well-defined software development technique to reduce software complexity, improve clarity and facilitate debugging and modification.
synchronous	A system in which each event, or the performance of any basic operation, is constrained to start on signals from a clock and usually to keep in step with them.
syntax	The rules governing sentence structure or statement structure in a language (natural language or formal language).
system	All items (e.g. people, procedures, hardware and software) organised to accomplish an identified function or group of functions.
system architecture	The structure and relationship among the components of a system. The system architecture may also include the system's interface with its operational environment.
system design	The process of defining the hardware and software architectures, components, modules, interfaces and data for a system to satisfy specified requirements.
system testing	The process of testing an integrated hardware and software system to verify that the system meets its specified requirements.
takeover	Usually the stage in the fulfilment of a contract at which the customer takes possession of equipment in terms of ownership and custody. It does not necessarily imply agreement that the equipment is satisfactory or complete. Contrast with *acceptance*.

task builder	A utility program provided for linking object program modules into a single executable program.
technique	A formal strategy for carrying out an identified activity or task.
test	The operation of a functional unit and comparison of its achieved result with the defined result to establish acceptability; for example, a device test or a program test.
testing	The process of exercising or evaluating a system or system component by manual or automatic means to verify that it satisfies specified requirements or to identify differences between expected and actual results.
throughput time	The time interval between the availability of all input parameters to a system process and the production of an output or result.
time-out	A time interval allotted for certain operations to occur.
tool	An aid for the performance of an identified activity or task. See *CASE tool* and *software tool*.
transducer	A device that transforms one form of energy into another, e.g. a thermocouple transforms temperature difference into a potential difference. Usually applied to devices which convert various physical parameters (temperature, pressure, speed, etc.) into electrical signals which can be fed into a computer system.
translator	A program that transforms a sequence of statements in one language into an equivalent sequence of statements in another language.
transparent functions	Functions executed by the hardware or standard software of a system without the need for the user to explicitly call them or even be aware of their existence.
turnkey	A contract in which an agent undertakes to furnish for a fixed price all materials and labour, and to do all the work needed to complete a system.
upgrade	To enhance or expand the functional capabilities of an operational system.
up-time	The period during which the system is functioning satisfactorily.
usability	The percentage of time for which a functional unit or system can be used.
utility (program)	A program that performs a routine task required by many users, e.g. handling data files, copying, sorting and merging.
validation	The process of evaluating a system at the end of the development process to ensure compliance with requirements.
VAN	Valued Added Network. A service that provides additional facilities through a network.
VDU	Visual Display Unit. A device used in a computer system to display textual or graphical information to the operator. Most VDUs are used in conjunction with a keyboard so that the operator can input information or call up various displays on the screen.

verification
The process of determining whether or not the products of at the end of a given phase in the development stage fulfil the requirements established during the previous phase. See also *validation*.

virtual storage
Temporary transfer of data and/or program statements between memory and backing stores which enables better use of hardware resources so that the number of multiple users can be increased and their access times improved.

WAN
Wide Area Network. A computer communication network linking geographically distant localities.

walk-through
A review process in which a designer leads one or more other members of the development team through a segment of design or code, while the other members comment on technique, style, possible errors, violation of development standards and other problems.

watchdog
Hardware or software to monitor the operation of a computer to ensure that it has completed some given task within a specified period of time.

WORM
Write Once Read Many times. A form of optical disk storage to/from which data may be written and read; however data may not be overwritten, and amended and new data are always written to previously unused portions of the disk.

X25
A CCIR protocol that specifies the message structure required by computers and terminals connected to packet switching networks.

Section Thirteen: Abbreviations

AQAP	Allied Quality Assurance Publication (NATO)
ASCII	American Standard Code for Information Interchange
BCD	Binary Coded Decimal
BS	British Standard
BSI	British Standards Institution
CAMAC	Computer Aided Measurement and Control (standard)
CASE	Computer Aided Software Engineering
CCIR	Comité Consultatif International de Radiocommunications
CCITT	Comité Consultatif International Télégraphique et Téléphonique
CD-ROM	Compact Disk Read Only Memory
EPROM	Erasable Programmable Read-Only Memory
FPS	Fixed Program System
FVS	Full Variability System
IEEE	Institute of Electrical and Electronics Engineers (USA)
IPSE	Integrated Project Support Environment
ISO	International Standards Organization
LAN	Local Area Network
LED	Light Emitting Diode
LVS	Limited Variability System
OCR	Optical Character Recognition
OSI	Open Systems Interconnection
PERT	Program Evaluation and Review Technique
PES	Programmable Electronic System
PLC	Programmable Logic Controller
POL	Problem Oriented Language
PROM	Programmable Read-Only Memory
QA	Quality Assurance
RAM	Random Access Memory
RF	Radio Frequency
ROM	Read Only Memory
SGML	Standard Generalised Markup Language
VAN	Value Added Network
VDU	Visual Display Unit
WAN	Wide Area Network
WORM	Write-Once Read-Only Memory Area

Index

Guidelines for the documentation of computer software for real time and interactive systems

(2nd edition, 1990)

The IEE Information Technology Standards Sub-Committee welcomes any comments which readers may have on this document and its use. These will be helpful in the preparation of future issues.

Please return this sheet with your comments to:

IEE
Technical Regulations Department
Savoy Place
London WC2R 0BL

Comments:

Name: Telephone No:

Address: